Hot Feet Around the Emerald Isle

After five weeks of travelling up the west coast Ian arrives in Ireland's fair city, Dublin, where the misguided purchase of a very cheap pair of boots render his already sore feet far too painful to walk on any more. So he decides to search for a nice comfortable backpackers hostel in which to rest them for a while. As he ventures into the Sunny Southeast he eventually settles for Kirwan House in Wexford Town, and finds that this wonderful little town has more to offer than just being the sunniest place in Ireland.

Ian Middleton

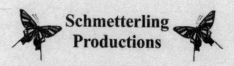

Schmetterling Productions

www.endofworld.co.uk

First published in Great Britain 2002.

Cover design by Stewart Middleton © 2002
Cartoons by Hans van Well © 2002

Published by Schmetterling Productions
ISBN 0-9540779-1-1
Email: schmetterling_productions@yahoo.co.uk
Website: www.endofworld.co.uk

Printed and bound in Great Britain.

Excerpt

Nervous Don and his wife were on holiday from Maine. I call him Nervous Don because Don was his name, obviously, and he was as nervous as hell when it came to driving on these tiny country roads. I didn't blame him really because after being used to the wide highways of America, the narrow, twisting lanes of County Cork must have come as quite a culture shock to him. Being on the other side of the road probably didn't help matters much either. Don was so tense behind that wheel that I suspected you would be unable to pull a needle out of his arse with a four-wheel drive.

One thing I was to discover in West Cork - and something Don and his wife were about to never forget for as long as they live - was the fact that all traffic, no matter what size, uses these country roads. As we approached a sharp turn a huge industrial dumper truck suddenly came hurtling around the corner and veered down upon us, taking up most of the road. Don impulsively swung the car into the hedge as his wife screamed, *'Oh my god!'* The truck zoomed on past and Don crept cautiously forward again, possibly in need of fresh underwear.

To the Kirwan House All Stars:
Butch, Davina, Éamonn, Richie, Eva,
'Scumbags' Sean, Widge and the unforgettable
Mr Marty McCool.

Contents

IRELAND

Tory I.

Bunbeg

Letterkenny

Belfast

Donegal

Sligo

Westport

Kilcock

Letterfrack

Clifden CONNEMARA

Galway

DUBLIN

Aran Is. BURREN

Doolin

MOHER

Wicklow

Kilkenny

Limerick

Wexford

Tralee

Waterford

Rosslare

Dingle

Tramore

Killarney

Blarney

Cork

Cobh

Glengarriff

Kinsale

Allihies BEARA Bantry

Durseyl. Skibbereen Clonakilty

Baltimore

1

A Pint of Murphy's, Please!

I wandered into the ship's bar in order to get my first real pint of Irish stout. Sure, I wasn't in Ireland yet, I was in the middle of the Irish Sea en-route to Cork. But I figured that as this ferry regularly docks in Cork then they should stock up with stout from there. An Irish barmaid from my hometown had reliably informed me that Cork is the city from where the Murphy's beer originates, and that it is the best in the world. I intended to find out.

Behind the bar stood a bloke who bore an uncanny resemblance to Uncle Albert (Only Fools and Horses). Showing through the thick mass of grey facial hair was a large grin. I expected his accent to be either Welsh or Irish, seeing as we had left Swansea for Ireland. But instead he spoke with a pronounced Scandinavian accent, and tended to waffle his words.

'A pint of Murphy's, please,' I said.

'*A pint of Murphy's!*' he exclaimed back, ringing a bell and then squeezing an air horn.

He then proceeded to pour it halfway, leave it and go serve someone else. I stood there momentarily confused. This was new to me. What the hell does he think he's doing? I thought. Had I been anything other than English I probably would have shouted, 'Hey just what the hell do you think you're doing? I was before him.' But we English are just too polite for that. We rarely complain about anything. If we do, it's done almost apologetically:

'Excuse me, I don't wish to be a pain but I did ask for a full pint of Murphy's and, well... I was first, you know. Could you possibly serve me before this gentleman?'

Despite the fact that we are paying good money for this drink, and therefore should get exactly what is ordered, we still feel guilty about having complained. Therefore I waited patiently while he served this other person, and watched as my half pint slowly began turning from fuzzy brown into a smooth jet-black colour inside its glass.

It was a good thing that I didn't complain because I was totally unaware of the fact that you have to wait for a real pint of stout to settle, and that to pour it properly it must be done in at least two goes; three is preferred. It was something I would be getting very used to over the next couple of months. (Looking back now, my fondest memory of an Irish pub contains a bar top lined with half filled pints of stout, waiting to settle, and a group of men armed with accordions, violins and guitars, playing folk music around a small corner table.)

When my pint was ready I took it over to the corner and sat down. Every few minutes the barman would ring that bell and honk that horn, which became increasingly annoying. However, I consoled myself with the sweet taste of the Murphy's.

I took a long swig of my pint and wiped the froth from my top lip. The thick, creamy liquid slid down my throat as smoothly as a milkshake. It was gorgeous. I now realised what I had been missing. The stout they serve back home is no patch on the real thing. There are many reasons for this, I was to discover. Firstly it doesn't travel well and therefore has to be brewed in England, and secondly, as it is brewed outside of Ireland, the water used is different. I don't know how - I always imagined water to be the same regardless of where it comes from - but it's apparently the reason why it doesn't taste as good. Also, my theory is that most draft beer in the UK is watered down in order to make it go further (more profit for the greedy).

As well as the fact that the beer tasted great, it was also cheaper: £1.70. So I drank another before wandering off to find a space on the crowded floor on which to spend the night.

Despite the journey being overnight many people, including myself, hadn't bothered to book accommodation. It was far cheaper that way. By the time I left the bar the ship was littered with bodies. People were sleeping on the floor, under the stairs and on chairs in the hallway. I wandered along the hall with a slightly pronounced swagger - which I put down to the motion of the ship and not the two pints of Murphy's I'd just consumed in the very short time I was in the bar - and on into the lounge bar at the rear of the ship. It seemed that just about every available piece of space on this ship contained a limp, snoring body. I soon found a vacant spot in the corner of the lounge area and lay my sleeping bag on the floor, then headed off to the toilet.

As I opened the cubical door and stepped inside, my foot hit something firm and sent me crashing down towards the floor, the toilet rim breaking my fall. Slightly dazed, I picked myself up to see that I had just tripped over a raised step at the entrance. On the top of that step, only visible once the door was open, was a sign that read: *mind the step*. I shook my head in disbelief and wondered whose clever idea it was to put a sign in a place where you would have to be looking down in order to see it, and therefore would have seen the step anyway. Interesting logic! I closed the door and proceeded to drain my bladder, then, mindful of the step this time, staggered the way back to my makeshift bed and settled down for the night.

The ferry docked at seven o'clock the next morning. I wandered off and out of the terminal to a red and white bus waiting outside. Bus Éireann (Irish Bus) is the name of Ireland's national bus service.

'How much to Cork?' I asked the driver.

'Tree pounds,' came the reply.

I love the way they say that!

I threw my bag into the luggage compartment underneath and found a seat towards the back. As the bus pulled out of the ferry terminal and drove on up the hill and on towards Cork, I made a circle in the condensation on the window and stared out at the rolling green landscape before me. My first day in Ireland, I thought, and it's raining.

I was about to embark upon a journey through what is affectionately known as the *Emerald Isle*. I didn't have a lot of money as this trip really hadn't been planned. About six weeks before, I had decided that I needed to embark upon another trip. Usually I plan to take these trips well in advance, and therefore am able to save well for them. But this time it was different. As a result I only had one month's wages and so I would have to make my money last as long as possible. I really knew nothing about Ireland – odd as it is right next door to my own country. But then you never really know anything about a place until you actually visit it. I had been strolling through my hometown debating where I could go on such short notice, and with such little money, when I bumped into an Irish girl I knew through a friend of mine. We chatted for a while and then parted company. It was then that it struck me. 'Ireland,' I said to myself. 'I'll go to Ireland.' It seemed logical. It was close and therefore wouldn't be costly to get to.

I thought back to all the Irish people I had met on my travels over the years and realised that there hadn't been a single one of them I had disliked. In Australia I had worked for a month with an Irishman, and we'd had such a laugh. The impression I had of the Irish was just that. They seemed to be very easy-going and fun-loving people who love to see the funny side of things. (The fact that Ireland's foremost television presenter, *Gay Byrne*, had been given a name which sounds more like an affliction among homosexuals, clearly shows this country has a sense of humour.) Testimony to that openness to fun was a book I now held in my hands called *Round Ireland with a Fridge*. The author, Tony Hawks, had hitch hiked round Ireland with a fridge in tow in order to win a crazy drunken bet. Over the month in question he was taken into the hearts of the Irish people who, it seemed, loved the whole crazy idea. Such an idea would be scoffed at by many, I'm sure. But not in Ireland, it seemed.

So with all that information, I had raked together all the money I could and boarded a boat for Cork. I had read in the guidebook that an estimated 35,000 people a year move to Cork, and that it has a considerable French input as a result of its ferry connections. If so many people were wanting to move there then there must be a good reason. Therefore I had decided to make it the starting point for my trip. I really didn't know much else about the country, but then I never really know much about the country I travel until I've travelled it. So as usual I just planned to start somewhere and see where the adventure would take me.

The bus dropped us off at the main station in the city centre of Cork, which was conveniently close to where I wanted to stay. I walked to a place called *Sheila's Hostel*, which was in a large building just across the main river that runs through the city. Among the many things on sale at reception I couldn't help noticing jars of Vegemite and packets of Tim Tams, seemingly confirming my suspicion, fuelled by the name, that Sheila's was run by Australians.

'No, it's run by an Irish woman called Sheila,' said the receptionist, after I had probed him on the subject.

'But why the Australian merchandise?' I asked.

'Oh, we get lots of Aussies coming through here, and they always ask for these things, so they decided to start selling them.'

He gave me a bed in a four-bed dorm and I ventured up a flight of stairs, dumped my pack down by the window, flopped on the bed and went straight back to sleep. I'm not one for early mornings.

__2__

<u>A Load of Blarney</u>

In all my travels the most important thing I have come to ask
of a hostel is a good shower. However, here at Sheila's I was
very disappointed indeed. It was 11.30 am when I finally rose
from my slumber and stumbled bleary-eyed through the hall-
ways of the hostel to the shower. The spray from the nozzle
was so spacious that even the most obese person would have
to move about to get wet. On top of that the hot water was
rationed to about five minutes. Still, I had no choice but to
attempt to cleanse as much of my body as I could with the
hot water, then use the cold water on the less tender spots.

Relatively clean and fresh again, I spent the afternoon
wandering around the city. What I saw shed absolutely no
light on why so many people want to come and live here. I
found Cork to be disappointingly rundown. It was like most
cities: smoggy, riddled with noisy traffic zooming along
roads that seemed to literally be cracking under the strain.
Also there was a dinginess about it. I was in the city centre,
yet it seemed more like I was on the outskirts. The rain had
stopped but the sky was still overcast, which didn't help

much. After a depressingly dull day wandering the city my spirits were immediately lifted as I re-entered my dorm.

The instant I stepped through the door I was greeted by the sight of a very attractive brunette sitting on the bunk above mine. She beamed a huge smile at me and instantly introduced herself: 'Hi there, my name's Shannon!'

I returned the courtesy and we got chatting.

Shannon was Canadian and travelling with a friend called Heather, who was a redhead. This was quite bizarre: two years earlier I had met two Canadian girls called Shannon and Heather at the start of my Mexico trip. Again they were a redhead and a brunette, only the other way round. Out of the two I had quite fancied Shannon. Out of these two I quite fancied Shannon also. But as before I would have no luck: Shannon and Heather were both leaving the next day. That's one of the downsides to travelling.

Still, before they did leave they invited me to go to the town of Blarney with them. Of course I gladly accepted. But first there was the small matter of having to leave the hostel. I discovered the next morning that this was a bank holiday weekend in Ireland and also the weekend of the Cork and Clare hurling match. Such a combination inevitably resulted in the hostel being booked out this day. As I had paid for only one night and not reserved the next I had to leave. I leafed through the guidebook and found the address of a hostel called Kinlay House. The guidebook said it was a friendly hostel but in a rundown area of the city. I figured that would be true of most places. So I threw on my backpack and headed off.

Along the way I was given directions by a very enthusiastic middle-aged man:

'Go up the steps now, and it's at the top by that church

with the big clock. It has four different faces, ye know. Also it's a wonderful view of the city from the top, now isn't it?'

I don't know, I thought, I haven't got there yet.

Another thing I was going to have to get used to was this very different way of talking.

Luckily Kinlay House had room for me, so I settled in and trotted off to meet the girls at the bus station.

Blarney village is situated about eight kilometres north-west of Cork. The main attraction is the kissing of the Blarney Stone. Blarney Castle was built on solid limestone way back in 1446. Situated at the top of this castle is the fabled Blarney Stone. Kissing this stone is reputed to give you the gift of the gab, or talk blarney as the term goes. Queen Elizabeth I invented the term because of Lord Blarney's ability to talk endlessly for hours without ever actually agreeing to her demands. Apparently his eloquent excuses for not surrendering himself and his land to her were so frequent and actually plausible that the queen declared his waffle a load of Blarney. It seems ironic that a well-known Irish expression was actually invented, not just by an Englishwoman, but by the English Queen who wreaked havoc on the country for years.

The castle is surrounded by some large and very beautiful gardens. As we wandered through these gardens on the way to the castle, it started to rain. This triggered the realisation that I had forgotten to pack the most important thing for this trip, *a raincoat*. How could I have been so stupid? I was about to go travelling in a country well known for its wet weather and I hadn't brought a raincoat with me. As Shannon and Heather put on theirs, I darted for cover.

The stone is extremely popular and is actually Ireland's third most popular tourist attraction. Thus there was a long queue of people waiting for their turn to smooch it. The queue stretched from the very top of the castle, six stories up, down a narrow spiral staircase and out the entrance. It was going to be a long wait.

Once we reached the top we were able to watch the kissing process. In the old days people who kissed the Blarney Stone were hung by their heels over the edge of the parapet. One day a pilgrim broke from the grasp of his friends and went hurtling downward to certain death. Nowadays bars are fitted to the inside of the parapet for the kisser to hold on to and thus be saved from the risk of falling down through the gap. Each person has to lie on his or her back and bend backward over a large gap on the inside edge of the parapet, which represents this sheer drop to the grounds below. However, this is obviously not considered safe enough. To further ensure the kisser's safety an assistant is provided. His job is to hold you by the waist as you bend over. Interesting job! It must make an amusing topic of conversation in the pub at night:

'So, what did you do today?'

'Well, I spent the day holding people's waists as they bent over backwards to kiss a stone.'

'Ah go on Seamus, now ye really ought ta stop these afternoon drinking sessions.'

It's not exactly the most romantic of jobs. Or is it? I suppose it depends on whose legs he's holding. I wondered if this one man was solely employed for this purpose, or whether the job was rotated among the park's staff?

Finally our turn came and each of us opted to take photos of this momentous occasion. I took one of Heather, then lay down myself, bent backwards, grabbed the two bars behind me and tried not to look down. The blood rushed to my head

The best job in the world?

as I stared at the smooth surface of the one stone set among other more rugged stones. I guess this is the Blarney Stone then, I thought. So what sort of kiss am I supposed to bestow upon this magical stone in order to be blessed with its magical powers? Do I just give it a peck, use a bit of tongue, or go for the full-blown Frenchy? It was a decision I would have to make very quickly, lest my assistant got bored and loosened his grip; or found something more interesting to look at. I figured this job didn't do much towards improving his attention span.

No one actually knows exactly where this stone came

from. There are various legends, but no real facts. It could have come from anywhere, and been anywhere come to think of it. But legend has it that if you kiss this stone you will be granted the gift of eloquence and inherit the ability to talk Blarney. I had read an article on the Internet stating that over the years the term Blarney has come to mean, 'The ability to influence and coax with fair words and soft speech without giving offence'

In the interests of decorum I decided to stick to a normal kiss, without tongue. After all, there was a crowd of people watching. Suddenly I realised that this was possibly not the healthiest thing I have ever done in my life: to kiss a stone to whom I hadn't even been introduced. And, come to think of it, to kiss a stone who has been kissed by thousands of other people: men, women and children alike. I would at least have preferred to get to know the stone better, taken it out for a drink first perhaps. But unfortunately for me there was no time allowed for a courtship ritual, so I had to dive straight in there and kiss this cold stone that was already dripping with the saliva of many before me. As I sat back up and allowed the blood to rush back to where it came from, I felt cheap, and extremely dizzy.

We spent the rest of the afternoon wandering around the castle gardens before catching a bus back to Cork. The girls had to catch the 3.15 train. Our bus arrived in Cork at three. Thus we said an extremely quick goodbye and the girls darted off towards the hostel to collect their bags. I hoped they would make it on time.

I had booked two nights at the hostel. I didn't fancy being kicked out again in the morning. I spent the rest of my time looking around the city and its suburbs. Although Cork itself was rundown, the suburbs weren't. Blarney had been quite a pleasant little village, and the small harbour town of Cobh (pronounced "cove") was very picturesque: a colourful place filled with buildings painted in various pastel colours. A train ran from the city and cost £2.50. The trip took about half an hour. Cobh's biggest claim to fame is that it was the last port of call for the Titanic before it met its fate in 1912. It's also a lovely quiet place to spend a sunny afternoon, which is exactly what I did. Well, an afternoon of occasional sunny spells.

I had decided to head off to Kinsale on Sunday. After my experience at Sheila's, I figured it might be best to phone the hostel the night before and book. It was fully booked. So I phoned the other. So was that. As they were the only two hostels there, I had no choice but to delay my trip a day. The owner of the first hostel had said there would be space on Monday. So I trotted off to reception to book another day here.

'Not a hope in hell,' was the receptionist's reply to my request. They were already overbooked. I wasn't having much luck really.

I decided that I ought to try and sort something out now, rather than wander the streets tomorrow looking homeless and dejected. I enquired in a hostel called Isaac's. They had space, but were expensive. I'd also heard bad things about them. So I told them I'd think about it. I shouldn't have been so choosy I know, seeing as I had been kicked out twice before. But I really didn't fancy staying there. The reception area was very formal, which made it quite impersonal. The guidebook stated that they make you vacate the hostel during the day. I hate those kind of hostels. If I'd wanted that sort of atmosphere, then I would stay in a hotel. I decided to try at

Sheila's again, on the off chance that they had at least one bed free. To my surprise they did. So I booked a dorm bed for the next day and then wandered off to find a decent pint of stout and some good live music. One thing Cork was well known for was its lively nightlife. I found a nice little bar which had a live band playing and enjoyed two of the things Ireland is most famous for: stout and music.

As I prepared to move to Sheila's the next morning, I got chatting to a group of men from County Clare. They had come down to watch the hurling match and had spent most of their time in the pub, by the sound of it. It was eleven in the morning and they were getting ready to head back off to the pub. They informed me that the landlord had told them to knock on the front door and he'd let them in, as they weren't officially open at that time of the morning.

After that I wandered over to Sheila's and checked in. This time I was put in a cramped six-bed dorm. Its only redeeming feature was the en-suite bathroom, although you had to fight your way over backpacks placed in the narrow gap between the bunks to get to it. I was glad I would be leaving the next day.

___3___

<u>Dangerous Country Roads</u>

Three people attempting to pack their bags in such a tiny space proved quite a feat. I lost count of the amount of times 'ooh sorry,' or, 'excuse me,' was said in the space of half an hour.

I took the bus to Kinsale and arrived forty-five minutes later. The hostel I wanted was on the other side of the harbour. The guidebook explained that a ferry ran from the Trident Hotel on the hour, so I wandered off in search of this hotel.

I found it a short way up the road, but there was no sign of a ferry. There was a series of mooring points along the harbour, but I had no idea from which one it was supposed to leave. So I asked a passing fisherman, but he knew nothing about it either.

'You can walk it in around half an hour. I do it quite often,' he said.

'I'll bet you've never had to do it with a bag like this,' I replied, pointing to my backpack.

'No I haven't,' he laughed. 'But I've done it with a few

beers, now.'

He directed me to follow the road up to the bridge, cross it and take a left.

I suspected that the fisherman had done this walk with those few beers inside him, because the walk took longer than half an hour. At the bridge I came across an apparently abandoned rowing boat and considered, just for a moment, borrowing it and rowing across. But it was chained up and had no oars, so I trudged on.

The hostel was beautiful. It was located in the picturesque *Castlepark Marina Centre*. Alongside it was a large shimmering harbour full of beautiful sailing and speed boats. I was put in a spacious dorm, the space being emphasised by the fact that I was the only one in there. But that would change later. Back at Sheila's, I had met Duncan from Melbourne. He had told me that he would be coming to Kinsale that afternoon, so we had agreed to meet at the hostel. Duncan was having trouble believing that the people here could be so friendly.

'I met this guy today,' he'd said as we were all sitting around a table in the dining room back at Sheila's, 'and he's offered to take me to Cobh tomorrow and then out in the evening for a few beers. What do you think? I mean, it sounds a bit strange, doesn't it?'

'It could just be a friendly offer,' said the American sitting with us.

'Yeah, but he said he would pay. It was the same back in Galway, an Irishman sat down next to me out of the blue and starting talking, then asked me if I wanted to go get a coffee. I mean, do I look gay or something?'

We all laughed. I must admit it was something I was going to have to get used to: the fact that people, men and women alike, would just start talking to you. The casual friendliness of strangers is not something many people are used to. Back home an offer like that from someone you'd never met would be treated with the utmost suspicion.

The Castlepark Marina Centre was nothing more than a hostel, a pub next door to the hostel and a marina out front. Any shopping had to be done in town, which meant that I would have to walk all the way back to where the bus had dropped me off. I sighed at my absent-mindedness. I should have thought about getting food before I set off over here. So I wearily trudged all the way back to town and spent most of the afternoon there.

Upon returning to the hostel I found Duncan had arrived. At the rear of the hostel was a small beach. It was hardly beach weather, as the sky was thick with clouds and the air quite chilly, but we figured it was worth a look. Duncan had a small rugby ball and suggested we have a throw about.

We set foot on the sand and were greeted by the sight of a very lovely Irish girl and her little Yorkshire terrier, Katie. Katie may have been small in size, but she was big when it came to guts. She spent her time chasing a large Labrador around the beach. Katie would race off across the sand snarling and growling at the Labrador, who in turn would run away. It seemed that size wasn't an issue in the Irish dog kingdom. However, Katie's owner became a little concerned about her safety and eventually took her away, much to our disappointment.

The Labrador then joined Duncan and me in our game of catch, uninvited I might add. We couldn't resist the temptation to tease him with the ball, waving it in front of him or just out of reach of his maximum jumping ability. This amusing game (well amusing to us anyway) continued for a good half hour. Inevitably the moment came when one of us misjudged our four-legged friend's ability and he got the ball. Thankfully it was Duncan who lost. The tables were turned and this time the dog refused to let go. Duncan spent the next fifteen minutes chasing him all around the beach, while I stood there laughing.

Duncan left for Kilkenny the next day, after we'd taken a walk to visit the ruins of the seventeenth century Charles Fort, and taken in its incredible harbour views. The son of the family who ran the hostel took us both across to town in his boat. This must have been the ferry the book had talked about.

The town of Kinsale is quite small but attracts many visitors in the summer. Its large harbour and many historic buildings makes it a very picturesque place indeed. It's also the undisputed gourmet capital of the world. Not being able to afford to find out I just had to take their word for it. Instead I bought some scraps from the supermarket and cooked them back at the hostel.

That evening I wandered into the *Dock Inn* next door, bought a pint of Murphy's and found a nice little corner. I pulled out my copy of *Round Ireland with a Fridge*. A friend back home had lent it to me on the proviso that I would collect a beer stain history of my trip around Ireland. It was just one of those stupid conversations you have - possibly fuelled by the author's silly bet.

'I'd lend it to you, but you'll probably get it covered with beer,' Allan had said.

'No I won't.'

'Yes you will.'

'Well how about I collect samples of different Irish beers

from different places in Ireland?'

'Hey that's a good idea,' he replied, his mouth spreading into a full blown grin. 'A beer stain history of your trip.'

And so it was settled. The only thing was that anyone seeing me do this might think I'm a bit crazy. I wouldn't blame them, I was beginning to think I was too. I sat there reading and looking around me for the right moment in which to furtively spill some of my pint in the back of the book. Of course once that was done I then had to allow it to dry. I couldn't blow on it, the family sitting at the next table would have definitely thought me a madman. After all, what would you think if you saw a bloke sitting alone in a corner blowing on the inside cover of a book? So I secreted the book by my side and slowly sipped my beer.

My other mission while in Ireland was to find the famous *Sisters of Murphy's*: the three stunningly gorgeous brunettes who prance around in black cat suits that look as though they have been spray-painted on over their lusciously curvaceous bodies. And they always seem to appear when a man's pint of Murphy's is in imminent danger of being spilt, and consequently save the pint. Anyone who's seen the advert will know exactly what I mean. Therefore I made a point of placing my pint precariously on the edge of the table in-between sips. They didn't show, so I figured I would just have to keep trying. Now that I've kissed the Blarney Stone I should have no problem seducing each of them in turn, or at the same time. After all, I now have the ability to influence and coax with fair words and soft speech without giving offence. Should come in very handy indeed.

When the stain was dry I wrote next to it the name of the beer, the town and pub it was bought in, and the date it was acquired. With that done I took my empty glass up to the bar for replenishment. My book sparked up conversation with one of the locals sitting at the bar. He remembered when the author was doing the trip. 'Ah yes, it was all over the radio,' he said.

I was then befriended by a toothless old Englishman from Portsmouth. He was part of a large group over here for a fishing holiday. They were spending their days out on a boat, and the evenings in this pub. I mentioned that I had never done any deep sea fishing before. In fact I was completely hopeless when it came to fishing altogether. They assured me that deep sea fishing was a lot more fun and offered me the chance to come along the next day. I had actually planned to leave then. But they said to think about it and if I wasn't up when they left then they'll assume the answer is no.

I awoke the next morning to the sound of the guys in the next dorm getting ready. I lay there thinking about what I should do: head off to Clonakilty or spend a day out on a boat with a bunch of extremely hungover Englishmen? No competition really: it was off to Clonakilty.

For the first time since my arrival in Ireland the weather was gorgeous. To get to Clonakilty by bus from here would entail taking one all the way back to Cork and then another back out to Clonakilty. The bus route I was on stopped here. Looking at the other route I saw that it stopped at Innishannon. If I could just get out to there then I could intercept the bus on its way through. The only option was to hitch. Now I'm not a huge fan of hitch hiking. Apart from the obvious reason – the local serial murderer doesn't wear a hat advertising the fact – I don't have the patience. I've only really done it once or twice before and it was fun, I must admit. But I don't think I'd use it as a regular mode of transport, just in situations such as this.

I made my way to the other side of the bridge where I had discovered the boat. If only that wasn't chained up, I thought. I could take it and row upriver to Innishannon. But that just wasn't possible, so I found a suitable spot, removed my back-pack and assumed the position.

This was the first time I had ever hitched alone and I must admit to being a little apprehensive. Also, I never realised how tiring it could be just standing there with your thumb sticking out. With each passing car that thumb slowly started to wilt. Half an hour passed and no one had stopped, so I decided that I would walk along as I hitched. At least that way I would be making some progress. Innishannon was only ten kilometres away and at worst I could walk all the way. Although, I had serious reservations about my fitness level allowing me to do this. I'm certainly not averse to walking, I do it quite often. But normally I'm not carrying such a heavy weight on my back in the process. Even so, I figured it better than standing around waiting for a lift that may never come, and so trotted off along the road.

Around the corner the road narrowed somewhat. This made it slightly difficult to hitch, especially when big trucks would come hurtling around the corner. I didn't dare stick out my thumb for fear of losing it. Because of this the drivers didn't think I was hitching and would just wave at me as they passed. I did manage to thumb the cars that passed. None of them stopped though. However one did pull in to a parking bay further down the road.

I refrained from running down after them, in case they hadn't actually stopped for me. It could have been quite embarrassing for all of us had I jumped into their car only to find they had just stopped to read a map. In the distance I could see a woman get out and take a photo. This confirmed my suspicion. But as I got closer I could see the driver beckoning me over with a wave of his hand.

'How far you goin?' came a distinctly American voice, as I arrived at the window.

I explained my situation and they both agreed to take me there. He made room in the boot for my backpack and then room in the back for me. They certainly had plenty of luggage.

Nervous Don and his wife were on holiday from Maine. I call him Nervous Don because Don was his name, obviously, and he was as nervous as hell when it came to driving on these tiny country roads. I didn't blame him really because after being used to the wide highways of America, the narrow, twisting lanes of County Cork must have come as quite a culture shock. Being on the other side of the road probably didn't help matters much either. Don was so tense behind that wheel that I suspected you would be unable to pull a needle out of his arse with a four-wheel drive.

They wanted to get to the Beara Peninsula in West Cork. As Don drove cautiously along the road I took the map and helped them out with directions. Their plan was to take the coastal road that, advantageously for me, went through Clonakilty.

'Well it looks like you'll get a lift all the way!' said Mrs Don.

If we ever make it there. They were completely lost.

'We can't seem to find the turn off for this coastal road,' explained Mrs Don.

I looked at their map. 'I think you've passed it,' I said. 'You need to turn around.'

So Don nervously turned the car around in the narrow

road and headed back the way we had come.

Unfortunately though, it soon began to look as though they had passed the turn off for that road way back before even meeting me. We followed the road back to where I was picked up and still there was no sign of the coastal road. I suspected that we just needed to go back to Kinsale and cross the river. However they weren't so optimistic, and so they both decided to continue on the way they had been going and take the inland road to the Beara Peninsula, much to my disappointment. I consulted the map and saw that their new route would take us through Bandon, a town further along the Bus Éireann route. I suggested they drop me off there. The further I could get the better. I noticed that the distances on the road signs were given in both kilometres and miles. From what I could work out, the old white signs were in miles while the modern green ones were in kilometres. Could cause confusion.

One thing I was to discover in West Cork - and something Don and his wife were about to never forget for as long as they live - was the fact that all traffic, no matter what size, uses these country roads. As we approached a sharp turn a huge industrial dumper truck suddenly came hurtling around the corner and veered down upon us, taking up most of the road. Don impulsively swung the car into the hedge as his wife screamed, *'Oh my god!'* The truck zoomed on past and Don crept cautiously forward again, possibly in need of fresh underwear.

We made it safely to Bandon and they dropped me by the side of the road. I thanked them for the lift and bade them both farewell, wishing them luck; I figured they'd need it. Somehow I suspected that pin would be even more difficult to pull out now.

I found the bus stop, sat down and waited. The bus was due through at midday, so I had about a half-hour wait. I couldn't help noticing that sitting at the bus stop on the other side of the road was an attractive brunette. I would have preferred her to be sitting here. Instead, it seemed I was stuck with the town drunk. Up staggered an old man wearing a dirty grey suit with a tie dangling from the bottom of his buttoned up jacket, from which his beer belly seemed to be desperately trying to escape. In his hand was a dirty old shopping bag, the kind your grandma was always carrying, and two packets of deli sandwiches. He slumped against the bus shelter, smiled at me with his big red face and then proceeded to munch his sandwiches. In-between bites he spoke. I couldn't for the life of me understand a word he was saying. Not only was his mouth full, but he spoke with the broad accent of a man from the countryside. At first I wasn't sure if he was speaking English.

'Ah, you'll be wayting fer de boos too, now will yer?'

I nodded.

'Ah see, whare yous froom?'

I nodded again, and added a nervous smile.

He spoke something similarly incomprehensible once again. Fortunately by this time a woman had come along and, obviously sensing by the scared look on my face that I couldn't understand him at all, kindly provided me with the translations.

Eventually the bus came. I tried to avoid him on the bus, but this proved fruitless.

'Ah, you'll be wahnting to sit here,' he said, beckoning me to the window seat next to him. He then got up to allow me in. 'I be getting off before ye.'

I thanked him and sat down.

During the trip I began to comprehend his accent, and learned that he lived in a small village nine miles from Bandon, where he owned a plot of land; twenty-five acres to be exact. A rich drunk, I thought.

As the bus pulled into Clonakilty I got off, only to discover that I couldn't open the luggage compartment door. The bus stop was in the main street, which like most villages wasn't very wide. It seemed that in this part of the world there was no law against parking in the bus lane; or at least that law wasn't adhered to. As a result our bus had to stop in the middle of the road. It was so close to the parked cars that one was in the way. I quickly rushed to tell the driver before he drove off with my bag, and he moved out slightly. I retrieved my backpack and hauled it on. Looking around me I was dismayed to see that all manner of traffic came zooming through this narrow village street: from cars to large buses and massive industrial trucks with wheels higher than the average car. These trucks wouldn't slowly pick their way past the parked cars, but would instead weave their way through without any apparent use of their brakes, like a rally driver late for his tea.

Upon arrival I found the hostel at Clonakilty was closed for cleaning. A sign at the window directed me to the B&B across the road. It was owned by the same people. I left my bag there and was told to come back after two o'clock. The town is situated in Clonakilty Bay, so I decided to pass the time there.

As I wandered down I pondered my day. It had been quite eventful really. I had walked, hitched and bussed my way here. The hitching had actually been quite a lot of fun. I also wondered what it would have been like had I not caught that lift and ended up walking to Innishannon? It would have been exhausting with the added weight of my backpack. But the thing is that backpacks are designed specifically for that purpose. When I thought about it, I'd never really walked any considerable distance with mine before. During my travels I had mostly caught a bus or train, then caught a local bus or taxi to the hostel, if it had been quite far. Therefore I wasn't really a true backpacker. In Mexico once, I had met a guy who would hike everywhere through the mountains with his pack. He was a rock carver and his pack was filled with stones he'd collected along the way. It weighed a ton, and he wasn't much bigger than me. With this in mind I decided that I should actually try to walk a significant distance with my pack in order to achieve the status of a true backpacker. My next destination was Skibbereen, so maybe I would walk there.

Enquiries at the hostel proved this to be a bad idea. It was twenty-two miles away. With my fitness level that was bordering on suicide. Instead I decided to set myself a personal challenge. At some point during my trip I would walk between two towns, hostel to hostel. On the strength of that I figured I ought to get some walking practice and also boost my fitness level – and believe me, it needed boosting. I consulted the guidebook and found that Inchydoney Beach was only five kilometres out of town, so I figured that to be a good start. A walk there and back ought to prove good training.

Along the way I passed a sign at the entrance to a field that read:

Temporary dwellings prohibited.

Interesting terminology.

Further down the road a car sped past, screeched to a halt and reversed back. The driver lent out of the window and then said, with a look of shock on his face: 'Oh I'm sorry! I tought yer were someone else. Nevermind, do yer want a spin anyway?'

I told him I was fine and that I was just walking to the beach. Under normal circumstances I would have taken the lift, but that would have defeated the object of improving my fitness for my impending hike.

'Are yer sure yer don't want a spin?' he asked again.

'No thanks I'm fine,' I replied.

So he sped off. The people are so friendly here, I thought to myself as I continued on down the road.

The majority of the latter half of the walk took me along the huge shallow inlet of Clonakilty Bay. The ebbing tide had left behind a vast landscape of large yellow sandbars. Inchydoney Beach was also large and very beautiful. So I plonked myself down on a sand dune and relaxed for a while before embarking on the long walk back.

It had taken one hour to walk there, and that was without my backpack. When I did take up my personal challenge I figured I'd have to give myself plenty of time.

When I got back to the hostel my feet were burning. So I spent the evening with them up on the sofa in the hostel's cosy living room, watching a video I found by the television. It was the film *Michael Collins*. A fitting film to be watching here. Michael Collins was born near Clonakilty, and played a big part in the liberation of the Irish Republic from Great Britain. It was also a good opportunity to learn some Irish history, albeit somewhat dramatised by Hollywood. I never realised just what atrocities the British government had committed on these people, until now. It certainly explained the political animosity between our countries.

__4__

Baltimore

I caught the ten past ten bus to Skibbereen the next morning. As I got on I befriended an old man and woman from Plymouth. Dermot had brought his sister over for a holiday.

Upon arrival I had the same trouble as before getting to my luggage. This time however, instead of moving out for me the driver got off and held the door open as far as he could without scratching the adjacent car, while I squeezed my pack through the gap.

The only hostel in Skibbereen was the *Russagh Mill Hostel* just outside of town; one and half kilometres to be exact. Another fitness test. I soon realised that whatever route I did take on my upcoming hike would have to avoid roads as much as possible. Mainly because walking along roads is really boring, so there is nothing to take your mind off the ache in your shoulders. I checked into my dorm, had a coffee and then walked back into town via a walking trail that started at the back of the hostel. There wasn't much around town so I decided to hop on a bus to Baltimore. Now there's a strange line to find in a book about Ireland. However this Baltimore is a small fishing town with a population of around 200. It's a well visited place in the summer, though. People come to sail, dive and visit the nearby islands.

Skibbereen's bus stop was a pub. Only in Ireland could this be possible. In the smaller places around the country the nearby building would act as an agent for the service. In most cases it would be a shop or a café, but here it was a pub. Obviously I had to go in and find out the time of the next bus. As I had a half-hour wait I figured I might as well have a pint of the Black Stuff. What is this country doing to me? I thought. It wasn't even midday and I was drinking. I only had one though and then got on the bus, closely followed by everyone else at the bar. It seemed that the owners weren't stupid when they agreed to act as a Bus Éireann agent. Dermot and his sister were on the bus too. I sat behind them and spent the journey waffling about my travels, mostly stimulated by the pint. They seemed quite interested though.

At Baltimore we all got off and most people caught a ferry over to Clear Island, Ireland's southernmost point. I was on a tight budget as usual, and decided to just take a walk along the surrounding coastline. A huge white concrete block dominated the hilltop just outside of town. From a distance it looked like a giant milk bottle. I soon found out that this giant milk bottle was actually a navigational beacon. Set at the entrance to Baltimore harbour this beacon has warmed the hearts of many a returning fisherman or sailor. Positioned high above the channel between the mainland and nearby Sherkin Island it's the image that is most often associated with the village.

I took a stroll up to it and along the cliff edges that dropped off into the jagged rocks and surf below – not a very sensible idea after just having a pint. It's not enough to cause drunkenness, I know. But it's enough to upset your sense of equilibrium.

The views from this area are magnificent. You can see the two islands, the harbour and the mouth of the Ilen River. You also get a good view of the village and the remains of the *O'Driscoll Castle* that dominate the village.

I then decided to walk back along the coastline instead of the road. It seemed like a simple task, but I was soon to discover otherwise. Further along I found myself trapped in by marshland. I couldn't continue and I didn't want to go all the way back. The marshland stretched out to a stone wall, so I figured if I could just get to that then I could walk along the wall. The only way across was to use the large clumps of grass as stepping stones. I took each step with a wobble and a fear of sinking into the mud. Finally I reached the wall and climbed on.

Immensely pleased with myself for having overcome this huge obstacle, I confidently dug in my heels and began to stroll on along the wall. Suddenly I found the wall begin to crumble under my feet. My legs split apart as both feet slid and tumbled down either side of the collapsing wall. I winced in pain as my crotch crashed heavily down onto the jagged rocks. It seemed that the stones had just been piled there and not cemented together. While I sat there for a moment waiting for the shooting pain to ease and my voice to return to its normal pitch, I noticed that the wall separated the marshland from the more firmer ground. So I jumped onto the grass and walked over to the road. I figured it best to continue along that way.

Back in Baltimore, Dermot and his sister had returned from the island. I found them having tea outside a pub over-

looking the small port, with a man they had met on the boat. Dermot told me his name was Michael, but when I called him that he replied, 'My name's Bill.'

Bill had been born in Ireland but grew up in Durham. When he retired he decided to return to the land of his birth. Like many, he had been forced to leave Ireland in his youth due to the lack of work. But he had always loved Ireland and as soon as he retired he had no hesitation in returning home. As a pensioner he gets free travel on all buses, trains and ferry rides like the one to Clear Island. He also gets free phone rental and many other perks. It seems that Ireland really looks after its elderly, even if you haven't been living there all your working life.

Back in Skibbereen I wandered into the pub to check the bus times to Bantry for the next day. I was closely followed by the others and Bill offered to buy me a beer. Well it would have been rude to refuse, wouldn't it? He called the others over and we had a drink while they waited for the bus back to Clonakilty.

The second pint had made me feel hungry, so I picked something up from the shop on the way back to the hostel. In the communal kitchen I set about preparing my gourmet meal of microwavable chicken steak sandwiches. Now, being an electronics technician you'd have thought that figuring out how to use a household appliance wouldn't have been all that difficult. Normally it wouldn't. However, this microwave was like something I'd never seen before. It was huge and I couldn't for the life of me figure out how to work it. On the front was a display and a row of numbered buttons. What any of these corresponded to was a mystery. Sheepishly I asked the other guy in the kitchen if he knew how to use it.

'It's an industrial one,' he explained, and proceeded to show me what to do.

Of course I knew that.

There was a distinct lack of utensils in this kitchen. I hate hostels like this. I couldn't find anything. As I slammed doors and huffed and cussed when I eventually found what I wanted in the place that it shouldn't be, the guy stood watching me.

'Christ, everything's all over the place in this bloody kitchen!' I said, becoming aware that he might be considering calling a member of staff to have me removed.

'This is the staff kitchen,' he replied.

'Oh!'

The industrial microwave should have given me the hint. It transpired that the guests' kitchen was downstairs, so I went there.

After eating I returned to my dorm. The hostel was fairly quiet. I was the only one in my room. I could hear some people moving around in the room next door, but I never saw them. It was around eight when I wandered out into the dining room. No one was there either. I stood and gazed out the window at the countryside ahead. It was a lovely view of rich green fields, trees and grazing cows. All of a sudden I found myself drifting into a mild state of euphoria. I felt more relaxed than I had felt in a long time. All the stresses I had known back home just melted away. I thought clearly for the first time about what I really wanted from life.

After years of travelling I had returned to England and this time tried to settle back down. I had listened too much to the people around me saying that it was about time I settled down, and begun to think that maybe they were right. I couldn't go on like this, working for a few months a year and then travelling, each time coming back and having to start again. But I loved travelling. I loved the adventure of it, the meeting of interesting and amusing people from all around the world, from whom I had learnt so much. I loved discovering new and wonderful places in the world. Even now I was just a week into this trip and I had met some amusing characters. Already this trip had renewed my enthusiasm for travelling and made me realise there and then that this was what I loved most. This was what I wanted to do, and would continue to write these books and somehow make a living from it. It would mean many compromises. It would mean that the road would be long and difficult. But I realised there and then that I had a choice: I could give up on my dreams and go back to being in a 'normal job', and end up bitter and depressed for the rest of my life, or I could chase that dream. Sure I may never succeed, but I will at least be trying, and doing what I love most in life. I might not make much money from it, but I could always supplement it with temporary work as I had been doing since my first ever trip to Australia. I had worked for a few months, saved all my money and gone travelling. However, instead of returning when money ran out and starting again, I would have to start building up a nest egg. This could ensure that no matter what happened I would always have something to fall back on. Instead of being a slave to the system, like I had been for years – relying on that monthly wage packet to live on – I would use the system to my own advantage. I would use my money more wisely in future and thus always allow myself the freedom to choose.

Feeling rather pleased with myself for making this momentous decision I snapped out of my delirium and suddenly became aware of an old man standing next to me.

'Where are you from?' he asked.

'Andover,' I replied.

His look quite clearly showed that he was trying his best to figure out where this place was in the world.

'Andover is a small town in the south of England,' I informed him.

It soon transpired that he hadn't been thinking about where it was, but was actually analysing the word. He then started waffling on about the English language. He proceeded to describe, in lengthy detail, how the word 'and' should be used in a sentence, and how it is used nowadays:

'You can use it many times now, even at the beginning of a sentence. Unlike before, you can even put two next to each other.'

He then went on to cite many different examples:

'Now you can say things like 'And I went to Southampton and Andover and had a great time.' All in one sentence.'

I could actually feel my brain cells shutting down one at a time.

Looking very pleased with himself he then went on to tell me how he was born in Manchester, grew up in Tipperary and went to work in Canada.

'I don't know where the hell I'm from,' he said.

I don't think you know where you are now, I thought.

Then as abruptly as he had appeared he was gone, leaving me seriously wondering about my sanity.

___5___

<u>Unofficial Closing Times</u>

Bantry's bus stop was situated in a more spacious part of the town, so this time I was able to get to my backpack without having to move the bus. I hauled it on and went off in search of the hostel, unaware that I was being closely followed by a French girl. When I stopped to ask directions at a garage, I noticed her appear alongside us. Sandrine was working on a farm near Clonakilty and made use of her weekends off to see some of the country. We followed the man's directions and after trudging up a steep hill we came to the *Bantry Independent Hostel* and checked in. This was definitely a quiet part of the country. Once again I had the dorm to myself.

The hostel was being run by Paul. As well as doing my laundry for four pounds, he also furnished me with plenty of information about the area. The south-western part of Ireland is made up of a series of peninsulas. Bantry is on the edge of the Sheep's Head Peninsula. Next up is the Beara Peninsula. Above that the Ring of Kerry. Paul told me about the Beara

Way, a walking track that goes right around the entire Beara Peninsula. It's 197 kilometres in total length. The terrain is wild, rocky and harsh. 'Perfect walking country,' explained Paul.

Sounds like a good place for my personal challenge.

It also sounded like an interesting place to visit. I remembered that Nervous Don and his wife had been heading over this way, and idly wondered if I would stumble across their car and find them both sitting rigid in the front seats, their faces contorted into grotesquely frightened looks; a final confrontation with another large truck having taken its last toll on their hearts. If so then I'd give them a decent burial, sing the American national anthem (I felt sure I could conjure up the words to at least the first two sentences) and afterwards have a couple of hamburgers. Then steal their rental car.

Two more French girls turned up at the hostel this day, along with an American called Ian. I hate it when people have the same name as me, it just causes confusion. We all ventured into town that evening in search of beer and traditional Irish music. Paul had said that there might be some music in a pub called the Snug, and gave us directions. There was no music. A rock and roll band was playing next door, but it was packed solid. So we wandered through the streets in search of something better.

As we passed one pub a drunk stumbled out the front door, put his hand on my shoulder and slurred, 'You're gonna take me home!'

I told him he'd have more luck finding his own way. He obviously agreed because, without uttering another word, he staggered off into the night.

We eventually settled on a pub in a quiet street. It was

filled with old men either speaking in Irish or very fast, either way I couldn't understand what was being said around the bar. I spotted a sign for Beamish on the counter and so ordered one.

'Ah no! Dis is a Beamish free house,' said the barman.

'But there's a sign for Beamish on the counter,' I replied, pointing to it.

The barman shook his head. 'Still, dis is a Beamish free house,'

So I settled for a Guinness.

Looking around me I wondered if this scene epitomised the traditional Irish pub. If so, then at least we'd found something traditional. But all of a sudden, almost as if to contradict what I was thinking, one of the old men at the bar began singing: *'Brown girl in the ring, tra la la la la!'*

'Oh come on, don't sing that crap,' I said. 'Sing something traditional.'

He immediately looked up from his pint and glared at me with a face like thunder. *'What's fucking wrong with dat den?'*

'Oh, it's just not very traditional,' I replied, immediately deciding to rejoin the others before a fight broke out. I wasn't looking for anything that traditional.

The next day I decided to go to Glengarriff, which was the starting point for the Beara Peninsula. In the pub the night before the French girls had mentioned that they had their own car and were driving to Killarney. When I awoke I thought I'd try to catch a lift with them. Unfortunately, Ian had beaten me to it. So not only had he stolen my name, but also my lift. Bastard! Mind you, Glengarriff was only sixteen kilometres away, so I decided to try hitching again. I waved goodbye to Sandrine, who was going back to her farm today, and walked to the main road.

As I was standing there with my thumb sticking out, I couldn't help noticing a silver Mercedes drive past with two gorgeous brunettes looking at me through the side window. They never stopped though, much to my disappointment.

Half an hour later I noticed a small Volkswagen camper van pull over to the side further down the road. An old couple got out and wandered off. They returned a short while later and the woman began beckoning me over.

'Are you going to Glengarriff?' I puffed as I got closer.

She nodded and opened the side door for me.

I threw in my pack and clambered in to the back seat. This was a piece of luck.

They were both from Holland and were spending their retirement travelling. They had bought this van and explained that they would often just camp by the side of the road or in a lay-by wherever they ended up. Although, as the woman explained, every now and then they need the comfort of a B&B. They were a lovely couple, and very inspiring. People like this are living proof that you can still live life to the full, even when you are old. A lot of people I talk to about this seem to worry too much about something going wrong with their health while away from home. But it's a lot better than sitting at home waiting to die, isn't it? I guess it just depends on how adventurous the person is. Some prefer the safety and comfort of their own nest, while others fly off in search of adventure. I hoped I would always be the latter.

These two also represented the latter. They planned to drive around the circumference of Ireland. The coastline between Bantry and Glengarriff was incredibly beautiful: lush green fields with rocky outcrops and a rugged coastline.

The road wound its way through tiny villages and past many shallow inlets and rivers. We passed through the amusingly named town of *Ballylickey* and soon after arrived in Glengarriff. The woman explained that they were taking a boat ride which left from the pier opposite the Eccles Hotel, on the outskirts of the town, out to Garnish Island. It's a tiny fifteen-hectare island containing an Italianate garden created by the early 20th century architect Harold Peto. He planted an array of exotic plants never before seen in Ireland.

I was dropped off just at the entrance to the pier. The old lady jumped out and proceeded to help me on with my backpack. I thanked them both for their kindness and started walking into town. A short way down the road a silver Mercedes passed me, screeched to a halt and reversed back. The passenger window wound down to reveal the two attractive brunettes from before.

'How far are you going?' said the girl in the driver's seat.

'Glengarriff,' I replied, rather reluctantly.

'Oh, so you're here then,' she said, while the other sat there with the most gorgeous smile on her face.

'Yes,' I replied, wishing I wasn't. 'But thanks anyway.'

'Hey no problem.'

And with that they bade me farewell with a wave of the hand, smiled sweetly and then drove on down the road and out of my life forever.

I sighed the biggest sigh of my life and continued walking into town, chiding myself for being such an idiot. 'Are you stupid?' I said to myself. 'You didn't have to go to Glengarriff. You could have got in that car and had the most amazing time with two gorgeous American girls, or got a lift to the next town.' One thing was for sure, now I would never know.

Glengarriff is a long, thin village with more choice of accommodation than shops it seemed. Paul had recommended *Murphy's Village Hostel*, and asked me to tell the owner that Paul from the Bantry hostel is still waiting for his flyers. I was greeted at the door by a very friendly, grey-haired American woman. Susan had married an Irishman and brought up her family here in Ireland. She and her husband Tony had moved here a few years before and started up this hostel. And a bloody good hostel it was too. The dorms were clean and very spacious. And it had the best showers I had ever known in a hostel. Susan explained that when she set up the hostel, she made sure that good showers were installed. She obviously understood the needs of the backpacker.

I wandered into the kitchen and befriended Manny and Loretta, who were sitting by a set of patio doors opening out onto a large balcony. Loretta was from Australia. Manny, short for Emmanuelle, was from Brittany and, as she emphasised, not France. She explained that the people of Brittany consider themselves independent from the French. This was largely due to their Celtic ties. Loretta explained that she was heading off to start a job in Cork City in a few days. Manny had another week before she returned to France. She wasn't looking forward to it. She loved it here so much that she didn't want to leave.

It seemed that the Beara Peninsula was a mecca for the walker. And it all started here in Glengarriff. Susan provided me with a leaflet outlining the nine different walking trails around the village. The girls were about to go on one and invited me along. I accepted.

The area surrounding Glengarriff was as beautiful as the trip up here. Behind the hostel was the Blue Pool Amenity Area. The village is situated in a small bay at the lower corner of the peninsula. Its sheltered position, coupled with the influence of the Gulf Stream, gives it an extremely mild climate. Inland from the village lies the 300-hectare oak and pine Glengarriff Woods, which was where we were going walking. The thick tree cover, plus the amount of rain, maintains very humid conditions in which ferns and mosses are able to grow. One of the many creatures that has made this place its home is, what is affectionately known as, *The Kerry Slug*, described in the guidebook as the 'aristocrat of slugs'. I wondered how a slimy creature such as this could have achieved such a status. It's only found here, in parts of Kerry and the Iberian Peninsula, and is coffee-coloured with cream spots. Ooh, sounds positively delightful! Somehow I didn't think I'd be busting a gut to search this out.

Our first destination was the *Lady Bantry's Lookout*. It was a steep, relatively long climb but rewarded us with a fantastic view of the woods and surrounding area. We could see over the bay area and the village, and the rocky terrain that leads off west into the start of the peninsula.

We spent some time up there, soaking up the views before making our way back down and beginning a long walk along one of the many trails. However, the girls had to cut short their walk because Loretta needed to catch a bus to Bantry to get some money. As there were no cash machines in the village, she had to go there. While there they intended to collect sea snails and mussels. It seemed that they did this daily and ate them for dinner. Manny also did this here in Glengarriff. She explained that there were plenty to be found around the Blue Pool area.

'Do you want to come with us?' asked Loretta.

I did actually. But as I had hitched all the way here to save money, it seemed a bit daft to go back down and up again by bus. They agreed and invited me to join them for dinner later. I accepted and offered to bring the wine.

I decided to finish the walk before returning. Earlier, Loretta had said that she had received a warning to be careful when walking around the woods. It appeared that hikers were going missing from here up to Galway. Police believed that the abductors were dressing as policemen and priests, in order to lull walkers into a false sense of security. Therefore they would either go willingly, or be caught off guard. I don't know about you, but a priest approaching me in the middle of the forest would instantly arouse my suspicions. Many stories of murder, kidnap and even one about them being sold as slaves to an Arab Sheikh were being circulated. Maybe they are being kidnapped, drugged and initiated into some sort of religious cult? It was an interesting theory and one that could be added to the many going round. As I continued with my walk, I made a point to keep an eye out for suspicious-looking priests with hypodermic needles. I didn't relish the idea of waking up in some strange commune wearing a white robe and being referred to as *Brother Ian.*

I had tried to convince Loretta that she could do the walk and still meet the bus in time, but she hadn't shared my faith. A good thing too, as it took me well over an hour to complete the trail – stopping twenty minutes for a serene moment, and an arty photo of myself perched on a rock overlooking the valley. At the end of the trail I jumped out on to the road, pleased with my progress – that is until I discovered that I was lost. Walking round in circles had completely disorientated me. As I stood on the road I scratched my head. I had absolutely no idea which direction would take me back to the village, so I had no choice but to guess; although given the size of the forest that guess could well mean the difference

Danger lurks in Glengarriff woods

between an evening of mussels, wine and the company of two very nice girls, or a night spent in the dark, damp forest with nothing to eat but raw coffee-coloured slugs with cream spots. I knew which I preferred.

All of a sudden it occurred to me just how easily I could get lost here. When you think about it these trails send you up and down and around in circles so much that it would be impossible not to lose your orientation. There are no real landmarks for you to take note of and say, 'Hey I remember passing that, now I know where I am.' It's all trees, nothing more. And let's face it, unless you are a sad muppet with no life and no chance of ever getting a girlfriend, you are hardly likely to have studied the tree kingdom so intently that you would be able to tell one tree distinctly from another. And if you are like me and come out here with no real map, no compass and absolutely no knowledge of wilderness hiking, you could end up seriously lost; especially if you decided to leave the trail under the misguided belief that you could take a short cut. After all, you only came out for a short day hike, it's not as though you are trekking into the Amazon. This was more than likely what really happened to all those hapless hikers from here up to Galway. It was nothing as ridiculous as being abducted by priests or policemen, or being sold to rich Middle-Eastern oil barrens as wenches or slaves. These people simply took a wrong turn, strayed from the marked trail or hiked further than they should have for the day, and were now wandering round and round in circles delirious from lack of food, or following the lights of an aeroplane at night believing it to be the north star.

I took a wild guess and headed downwards, mainly because it would be less tiring than going up. A short way down the road I saw a sign advertising a river walk that took an average of twenty-five minutes. So in a moment of wild impulsiveness (fuelled by no other real idea of what to do) I took that, and soon found my bearings again. The walk took me along a crystal clear river and eventually on to the main road that led back to the village, much to my relief, where I bought that bottle of wine and enjoyed a very pleasant evening indeed.

*

The weather the next day was gorgeous. I found a nice quiet spot by the bay and pondered my next move. Adrigole was the next town along the peninsula. Tony had reliably informed me that it was exactly ten miles to the very nice new hostel there, along the Beara Way. Ten miles wasn't too bad a distance, I thought. I probably wouldn't get a better chance than this, so I decided upon this to be my personal challenge. I would walk all the way from this hostel to the hostel in Adrigole with my backpack and all its contents.

Back at Murphy's there was a new arrival in my dorm. Morris, from Newcastle, was also a writer and we discussed this along with the decline of social behaviour in the UK. It was hard going, not because of the topic but because he spoke so quietly. It was difficult to hear what he was saying. Later on, along with some other arrivals, we went to the interestingly named pub *The Blue Loo* for a late night drink. I was surprised to see that children were happily playing in this pub, while the parents drank. We left at 12.30 am, but not before I had annoyed the barmaid by wanting another drink. The official closing time in Ireland is 11.30-12.00 pm. The unofficial closing time, it seemed, is whenever the landlord feels he wants to, or can get away with. This was hardest on the bar staff, I think.

_____5_____

A Real Backpacker for a Day

I woke up to clouds closely followed by rain, hampering my chances of taking the hike. I would just have to wait until tomorrow. I spent the day discussing my planned walk with the people in the hostel. Most of them thought I was mad. They were probably right.

'I am bored, but not that bored,' said Manny.

However the more I outlined the pros and cons of it, the more she came round to the idea. Throughout the day she was going one minute and not the next. She eventually went to bed saying that if she was up, she would come. Knowing her track record of getting up early the past couple of days, I took that as a 'no'.

I was right. However, two Swiss-German girls had been convinced. But they left their main packs here in Glengarriff and took what they would need for a few days on the Beara Peninsula in a daypack. A much more sensible idea. But I had set myself a personal challenge and had to adhere to it. The weather had improved. It was still cloudy, but at least it

A real backpacker!!

wasn't raining. In fact this was perfect weather for hiking with a dead weight on your back. Imagine what it would be like with the sun beating down. After popping to the shop to get some food for the trip – two Chunky Kit Kats (I considered the hike to take four to five hours at the most) – I met the girls at the hostel entrance and we set off.

Beatrice and Bettina proved to be very enjoyable company indeed. They both had a fantastic sense of humour, and this proved to be the very thing that kept me going. The 197-kilometre Beara Way walking trail links Glengarriff with Kenmare (in actuality just twenty miles north of Glengarriff) via the entire peninsula, including the islands of Bere and Dursey. The trail leads along the southern half to the islands and then back along the north.

The first mile of the trail took us along the main road, from where it branched off on to a grass country road. We took a five-minute breather at this point. That hadn't been too bad. I had been so busy talking and laughing with the girls that I had hardly paid any attention to the weight on my back.

The trail led on past a farmhouse being guarded by a dog, but he soon moved at the approach of a man with a dead weight on his back and a crazed look in his eyes. Past the farmhouse we found ourselves heading in to the mountains. Stretching out before us was a rolling rugged terrain covered with sheep and their discarded faeces. Sugarloaf Mountain formed the backdrop. At 581 metres it was hardly a mountain, but low cloud level gave it an impression to the contrary. A few miles later we stopped for a bite to eat. The girls had packed a much more sensible lunch than me. Despite this I chewed on one of my Kit Kats and surveyed the area. I felt surprisingly good considering. Perhaps that walk back at Clonakilty had helped put me in shape. But I felt sure that the company I was keeping helped more. Having two people to talk to helps stave off the boredom, which in turn keeps the adrenaline pumping.

After our snack break we carried on. Before leaving, I had considered that the trip would end in one of two ways: I could either be triumphant, reaching the hostel fitter and with everything intact, or I could get completely lost in the mountains and collapse with exhaustion and dehydration – and join that list of people who have mysteriously disappeared. I imagined some twenty-fifth century palaeontologist excavating a skeleton with a backpack, and putting me in a museum to be known to millions as *Twentieth Century Backpacking Man*.

So far it was looking more like it would be the former. Before we left, Tony had given us very good directions and diligently shown, with the use of a map on the hostel wall, where to go. Unfortunately we couldn't take the map with us. Instead, Beatrice had drawn a very crude copy of it, which didn't really help that much. I'd never seen trees drawn like that.

We hiked on through a forest before turning off on to a narrow, marshy track that led up and over a pass along the edge of the mountain. It seemed that after the rains this track was also a route off the mountain for the water. As it had rained the previous day the ground now felt like a wet sponge. For the next half hour we squidged and puffed our way uphill and were rewarded with a breathtaking view at the brow of the hill. The rocky landscape rolled off into a shimmering pale ocean. It was an awesome sight. Somehow this seemed to compensate for my tiredness and gave me a second wind. To the west of us lay Hungry Hill. At 686 metres it's the highest point on the peninsula. Its name also brought on the realisation that I too was hungry, so we collectively agreed that this was a good spot in which to have dinner.

We soon realised that this was a hasty decision on our part. Coming over the hill had exposed us to offshore winds. As this wind came into contact with the sweat I had worked up while climbing the hill it sent a shiver that started at my head and vibrated violently through the rest of my body, eventually exiting through my toes. In a moment of desperation I considered shearing a few of the sheep wandering around and throwing together a nice fleece suit. But all I had in my backpack was a small pair of scissors, and figured this method to be a bit time consuming. So instead I took shelter behind a small hill, munched on my last Kit Kat and silently berated myself for not bringing anything at all to drink.

My philosophy when travelling has always been to just choose a country and drift round it, making things up as I go along and generally going with the flow. Up until now that philosophy has worked well, and proved to be the best and most adventurous way of travelling. But I really should learn to plan things like this a little better. I had been so absorbed with the whole idea of doing this that I hadn't really stopped to think just what I would need. My impulsiveness and eagerness to just do these sort of things without planning too much will one day get me into serious trouble, of that I've no doubt.* I looked up at the sky, it was still cloudy. Even given my reminder back at Blarney Castle I still hadn't thought to buy a raincoat. Had it decided to rain on us this day I would have been in deep trouble. There was no real shelter along this trail, except the small forest we had just passed through way back before climbing Sugarloaf Mountain. But that was behind us now.

Rested and fed, we continued onwards. We had hiked another mile or so along the narrow trails and over small streams when I had a sort of poignant moment with a sheep. (No, not in that sense.) Up until now, most of the sheep in the

*Find out how this came true on a 7-day hike in Patagonia, told in chapter 5, *The Pendulum* in the book To the End of the World and Back (A Millennium Adventure)

Man to sheep!!

way had scurried off at our approach and not looked back. But this one slowly moved to the side and regarded me with an obvious curiosity. We eyed each other for a moment, man to sheep. A kind of mutual respect passed between us. Then he shit down the back of his legs and trotted off.

I trudged onward, feeling the beginnings of an aching sensation in my shoulders. A bit further along, the trail rejoined the country road. Much of the Beara Peninsula is littered with prehistoric rocks, stone circles and old tombs. Beatrice and Bettina had been on the lookout for things called a *Standing Stone and a Wedge Grave*. I had no idea what they were, and quite frankly didn't care. When we came across one they trotted off across the field for a closer look, while I elected to remain behind and take advantage of the opportunity for the much-needed expulsion of bodily gases.

As I sat on the wall, pondering our progress so far - whilst raising a cheek every now and then - I noticed a big white dog in the distance bounding up the road towards me; possibly attracted by the smell. In a matter of seconds he was upon me and, after allowing me to pet him for a while, made the most impressive leap over the wall where I was sitting. He then ran off to where the girls were.

When we continued down the road the dog accompanied us until we reached his house. Standing outside was his owner, an Englishman who was born in Ireland and had decided to return here for his retirement. He explained that Max, the dog, would often sprint up to welcome the people who hiked this part of the trail. Feeling this was a good opportunity for a position check, I asked him how much further it was to Adrigole.

'About three miles,' he replied. 'It usually takes me about an hour. Are you going to stay at the hostel?'

'That's right,' I replied.

'Ah! I know it. It's a nice hostel. It's new, you know?'

I had heard that.

We refused his kind offer of a cup of tea and trudged onwards. About a mile or so down the road we came to a T-junction. The Beara Way sign that had so faithfully led us this far, pointed down the road. Next to it was a sign indicating that Adrigole was only three kilometres away. Our delight was obvious.

Halfway down the road we came across a house with two small cats and a dog eagerly waiting to greet us. The dog's cute face and wagging tail was an invitation for a break that we couldn't refuse. However when it came time to leave him, he wasn't so keen on that. He followed us all the way to the crossroads at the bottom of the road. It seems even the dogs are friendly in Ireland.

To the right, the road stretched off into the countryside. To the left, all I could see was a petrol station. Across the road was a cul de sac and a group of workmen. There were no signposts anywhere, so I crossed over and asked one of the workmen: 'Where is Adrigole?'

'Dis is it,' he replied.

'But where is the town?' I asked.

He pointed towards the petrol station and continued working.

We walked down to there and I asked inside.

'Dere's no actual town,' replied the lady behind the counter. 'It's just an area.'

An area as it turned out that was six miles long with a small scattering of houses. Obviously the inhabitants liked their space, or didn't like each other. I asked about the hostel.

'Oh it's about tree miles back that way, so it is,' she said, pointing the way we had just come. 'It's a nice hostel. It's new, you know?'

Yes I did know that.

I emerged looking extremely pale and told the girls the bad news.

'You don't want to hitch?' asked Beatrice.

I did want to hitch; I wanted to hitch badly. But this was a personal challenge, and the challenge was for me to walk from hostel to hostel. The taking of a lift in any form would represent failure on my part.

'You men and your personal challenges!' said the girls, in a manner which betrayed the fact that this was not the first time they had had this sort of trouble from a man's stubbornness.

I told them that they could go on ahead and hitch and I would meet them at the hostel. So they did. Huh! So much for moral support. I held back in order not to make it look as though there were three of us hitching. But further along the road I came across them sitting at the roadside looking defeated.

'No one will pick us up!'

We were all dead tired by this time. Personally, I felt like I had gone twelve rounds with Lennox Lewis and was having to carry him on my shoulders on his victory parade.

Our milestones came in the form of local people. The first came from an old couple standing by the road outside their house.

'Only two more miles. It's a nice hostel. It's new, you know?'

I was beginning to wonder if they were being paid to say that.

We were on the main road now, so the rest breaks became more frequent. Morale was low, but somehow we still managed to make a joke of it. This five hour hike was turning into a lot more than that. The afternoon had gone and it was well into the evening now. It wouldn't be long before the sun went down. Still, at least the rain had held off. I suppose we should have been thankful for that.

As we trudged past a shop, hoping that we were now fairly close, I asked a couple of men standing outside. They were eyeing us with amusement.

'How far is the hostel?'

'Just another mile, nice hostel, new!'

I wanted to throw my backpack at them and tell them quite articulately, whilst firmly gripping their throats, that I couldn't give a toss if it was new, I just wanted to get there while I still had a heartbeat. But I didn't have the energy. And it wasn't their fault, it was mine for having believed that I could actually undertake such a hike. What was I thinking? As I crawled down the road on my hands and knees, I chided myself for being such an idiot, and, worst of all, for subjecting two poor innocent Swiss girls to this. From behind I could hear the sound of a woman humming a sweet tune. Was I going mad and hearing things? No, it appeared that Beatrice had gone mad, as it was she who was humming. She laughed when we approached her about our concerns for her sanity and explained that it was the only way to take her mind off the fact that her whole body hurt. I had to commend these two girls for remaining in incredibly good spirits, even now when they should have been lynching me for persuading them to come along.

Half an hour down the road a car pulled up beside us and the driver asked if we were going to the hostel. He explained that he was the owner and had to pop out for a while, but to make ourselves at home and he'd be back shortly.

'Are we nearly there?' we asked.

'It's about a mile,' came the reply.

The three of us burst into a kind of insane laughter.

Fortunately that was just a very bad estimate on his part, and it was about half of that. Patrick explained that once we reached the bridge then it was about five minutes from there, and that we should call in at the shop along the way for our food. *Food!* I hadn't given it much thought, until now. And now my stomach started rumbling and I had hunger added to my bodily pains.

Once we reached the bridge we did a little dance of joy that resembled a trio of pensioners attempting to do an Irish jig. *'The bridge!'* we chanted, almost like a man reaching water after being lost in the desert for days.

We hobbled on, and as we approached the shop the old man standing outside regarded us with an amused look on his face.

'Ah now, what do ye tink you're doing?' he said to me. 'You've two strong women wit ya, and dey make ye carry de baggage.'

'So much for equal rights,' I replied.

The next ten minutes were spent in humorous banter about women making the man always do the work. The old boy ended the conversation with a very profound and extremely appropriate sentence:

'Ah well, you've got a good sense of humour and that'll always keep ye going.'

And how right he was. It was that sense of humour we all shared that had kept us going through this whole experience. Even when we were virtually on our hands and knees with exhaustion, we had still managed to laugh and joke about our situation. Without that, there might have been three skeletons to be found.

In the shop we bought ourselves food for the rest of the evening. I for one had no intention of doing any more walking tonight; except to the pub outside the hostel. As I paid the old lady serving at the counter, I suddenly realised she was mirroring my movements. She looked to be about ninety, and I had a sudden insight into how it must feel to be old. Each move I made repaid me with a sharp pain. My whole body hurt and I moved like an ape on valium.

It was now nine o'clock, so my theory about the walk only taking about five hours was completely blown out the window. In actuality it had taken nine. We found out later that we had taken a wrong turn and in fact should have gone straight ahead at that T-junction. Consequently we had added a few more miles on to an already long trip by walking down to the main road.

At the hostel I found the nearest bed, threw down my pack and feebly declared my victory, raising my arms and emitting a croak of delight. I had achieved my ambition and become a true backpacker for a day. I had literally farted in the face of adversity and not given up despite an intense desire to do just that; even if there had been no choice due to there being no way out other than to continue walking here. But I'd like to think I would have resisted had the owner of this hostel offered to turn his car around and give us a lift the rest of the way. Still, regardless of all that, my personal challenge had been met and beaten.

'You are a man now,' said Bettina.

'Yes I am,' I replied.

I then collapsed on the bed and groaned as my body convulsed and screamed in agony.

After a short rest period we showered, ate and hobbled to the *Glenbrook Bar* next door. The entrance was hidden around the corner. All was quiet. I cautiously opened the door and peered in. The bar area was devoid of life. As I looked to my left, I saw an old man sitting in front of a TV. A woman poked her head around the corner and beckoned us in. It appeared we were the first custom of the evening. It was eleven o'clock.

We went up to the bar and I ordered a pint of Beamish. As the iron from the stout rushed to feed the depleted muscles in my body, the old lady sat and chatted with us, whilst behind the shelter of the beer pumps I furtively added another stain to the collection in the back of my book. Somehow I felt the old lady really wouldn't understand. I'm still not sure I do.

'Where is everybody?' I asked.

'Ah, it's still early,' she replied. 'Dey won't start coming in until around eleven-tirty.'

Closing time was at twelve, officially.

Almost on cue, when 11.30 came, the local countrymen, all dressed in thick Aran jumpers and wellington boots, sauntered in one by one and converged around the bar. I had the sneaking suspicion that each of these men went to bed with his wife, waited until she was asleep, and then crept out to the pub.

___7___

Early Buses

Ironically, I had slept very badly. I would have thought that after a day like the one I'd just had I would have been out like a light as soon as my head hit that pillow. On the contrary, I'd spent a very uncomfortable night tossing and turning and drifting in and out of consciousness. Surprisingly though, when I got up the next morning I felt as though someone had swapped my body during the night for a new one. There wasn't a single ache left in any of my limbs and I felt as if I could do it all over again. Conclusive proof that Irish stout is indeed good for you. A perfect excuse to keep drinking it. My only disappointment was that this new, healthy body still contained an ever-growing pot belly. Somehow I felt that the stout wouldn't help improve things in that area.

After a refreshing shower I wandered into the dining room to find the girls looking equally fresh and having breakfast. We were the only people in the hostel. It was indeed new, like the many locals had kept informing us. Patrick had bought the old hostel that had once stood here and had it completely demolished. Apparently it was a complete dump. He then had this one built in its place. Patrick had been born in Liverpool to Irish parents. In his time he had done a fair bit of travelling and met his wife in Boston. His family had come from this area and so they decided to come and live here. As well as a nice new hostel, he also had the cheapest Internet access in Ireland. At the time he was just setting up and only charged us fifty pence. Most places I had used so far had been charging five pounds an hour. I told him about these extortionate prices and so he decided that once it was up and running he would only charge half that. Good man!

Castletownberehaven not only has the longest name in Ireland – alongside Newtownmountkennedy in County Wicklow – but was also our next destination. A bus ran there from Glengarriff twice a week. Fortunately for us, today was one of those days. It was due at quarter past twelve. It was close to twelve o'clock now, so the girls rushed on ahead while I finished sending some emails. I then grabbed my bag and set off to join them.

The bus stop was opposite the shop. As I left the hostel and trotted down the driveway, I watched in dismay as the all too familiar red and white bus shot past on the road out front. It was only five past twelve. There must be some mistake. Maybe it was an extra bus. I found the girls standing outside the shop with a look of total bewilderment on their faces. It appeared that had been our bus and that it had indeed come early. Who ever heard of missing a bus because it was early? Especially in Ireland where, I was rapidly finding, everything was so laid back. Most people miss a bus because they are late. But here on the Beara Peninsula it seemed you'll miss it because you are not early enough.

As that was the only bus of the day, and another wasn't due for a couple of days, we had no choice but to seek alternative transport. Castletownbere, as it's called for short (it's not really that much shorter, I know. But it's what the locals call it), was seventeen kilometres away. No, I wasn't going to walk it: one personal challenge in a lifetime is enough for me. Also Patrick had told us that the walking track between here and Castletownbere was extremely hard going after the rains. So the next option was to hitch. Three people, each with baggage, would present difficulty when it came to hitching a lift. Nevertheless we tried anyway. First we hid the baggage. Then we even hid some of us. Despite our efforts the cars still drove on past.

The old lady in the shop had obviously been watching and hobbled over after a while to tell us that we were wasting our time. 'The people won't pick up around here,' she said. 'They are afraid of being robbed.'

I don't suppose I could blame them really. After all, the hitch hiker isn't the only one who takes the risk.

We sat down and pondered our next move. We had pretty much exhausted all our options other than walking, which was an option none of us were keen on. Then Beatrice came up with an excellent idea: 'We should offer Patrick three pounds each to take us there in his car.'

It wouldn't hurt to ask, I thought. And I suspected he could do with the money, if business at the hostel was as slow as it appeared. So we trotted back down the road to the hostel. Patrick happily agreed to our request.

The one advantage to this mode of transport was that we got dropped off at the door of our next hostel, which was three kilometres past the town. As we pulled up out front we were greeted by a grey-haired, scruffy-looking old man wearing just a white vest and black trousers. Hans was from Germany and instantly began conversing in that language with the girls, while I stood there feeling as useless as a eunuch in a sperm bank. He then proceeded to give us all a tour of the hostel and its facilities, and a rundown of the hostel rules, in German. At least I had an excuse if I broke them.

The one downfall to the hostel was its distance from town. However, as we were now accomplished walkers this should not present too much of a problem. The dormitories were situated in wooden cabins out back. In the huge surrounding garden stood a selection of mobile homes housing a few permanent residents. As I wandered into the kitchen I got talking to one of them, a young Irishman with dreadlocked hair who explained that he had lived on the site for the past four years. It seemed that he hadn't washed his hair or clothes for that long either. He made no mention of what he did for a living, but he did give me the low-down on the area though, and about Ireland in general.

'Ireland is the paedophile capital of the world,' he announced, suddenly.

A fact that astonished me, if it were true. Let's not forget that this information was coming from a dreadlocked man who lived in a caravan in a remote part of the country.

He went on to explain that the Catholic church made a good job of covering up the fact that a vast majority of its priests were committing these atrocities on many of the young children in their schools and homes.

I didn't quite know what to say to this, so I made a cup of tea; the British answer to any situation where you find yourself speechless. It doesn't matter what has happened: say someone rushes home to announce that a nuclear missile has been launched on England and is heading straight for you and everyone will be obliterated. In the ensuing panic you can guarantee that someone will say: 'I'll go make a cup of tea.' Okay maybe that's a slight exaggeration, but you catch my drift. You'd think that tea represents a calming influence on these situations. But what it actually represents is a diversion, an excuse for a man not to get involved when his neighbour's wife runs into the house crying that her husband has left her, for example, or in my case a reason to change the subject. So I filled the kettle.

'What is it about you English?' he said. 'All the English that stay here put far too much water in the kettle.'

It seemed I had succeeded in changing the subject.

'How much tea are you making?' he asked.

'Just one cup.'

'Then why not put enough water in for one cup instead of wasting all that water?'

'Well, I'm sure someone will use the rest,' I replied, rather sheepishly.

'No they won't. They'll pour the rest away and fill it with fresh water just like you did.'

So I had. I had to admit that he had a point. I made my tea and then made a hasty exit.

It seemed there was a tourism war going on between here and Adrigole. When Patrick had dropped us off he'd left a box of flyers for his hostel with Hans. It soon transpired that Hans' wife had torn them up and thrown them in the bin. The reason being that the map on the back of the flyer hadn't shown Castletownbere. Oh dear me! The war of small minds on a small peninsula.

The girls and I spent the rest of the afternoon at Dunboy Castle. Not much remains of the castle now. It was once the fortress of the O'Sullivan clan, who ruled supreme for three centuries before finally being ousted by the English in 1602, by an army of 4000 men. However, plenty remains of Puxley Mansion, even though it was burnt down in 1921 by the old IRA. It was built in the nineteenth century with money generated by copper that had been mined by the Puxley family. Now it seemed it was home to a bunch of cows. The setting was beautiful. A path led us along a warm sheltered bay and then onto a circular trail that took us back to the mansion via the woods. All for the bargain entrance fee of 50p.

Despite our newly acquired skills for walking, we decided to hire some bikes and cycle into town instead. Also, we intended to use them the next day for a ride around the peninsula. Hans had a selection in his shed, which he hired for £8 per day. He explained, to the girls, that the hire price was for twenty-four hours and therefore we could use them to go into town. A good idea.

Castletownbere is Ireland's largest whitefish port. It's the main town on the peninsula, but still relatively small with one traffic-choked street and a main square. We rode in and treated ourselves to a sit down meal and a bottle of wine. After the meal we went off in search of a pub that Hans had recommended. McCarthy's pub was unlike any I'd ever seen before. Once through the front door we found ourselves in a shop. All around us were shelves of tinned food and other such consumables. Attached to the rear of the shop was the pub. So we wandered through and found a seat at the bar. The light was low and the wooden décor seemed fitting for such a small place.

After a refreshing pint of Murphy's we rode back to the

hostel, in the dark. It was a hair-raising ride along the narrow, dark country road, enhanced by the beer and wine. We sped on down the road trying our best to see the turns in time to make them. As we rounded a corner near to the hostel, the shadow of a huge beast came racing through a gap in the adjacent field and bounded straight for us. My heart jumped up into my mouth as I slammed on the brakes, skidded to a halt and remained there frozen as it galloped towards me, eventually revealing itself to be just a large horse closely followed by a donkey.

It's strong stuff that Murphy's.

8

Gluttons for Punishment

In the morning Hans laid on a typically German breakfast before pottering off to scrub the hostel clean. One thing about having Germans running the hostel was that the place was immaculate and well organised. So well organised in fact that as I was late for breakfast – I had slept through my alarm – mine was now cold.

Today we were to embark upon another gruelling adventure. We were going to cycle forty miles. We didn't know this at the time. If we had we might have thought twice about revising our plans – well I would have anyway. We wanted to visit the tip of the peninsula and a town called Allihies. Hans explained, to the girls, that we should go anticlockwise. This would mean that the last leg of our journey would be down a nice big hill. That's all well and good, I thought, but you have to get up that hill first. The word hill was soon to become an unpopular one in my vocabulary.

The first leg of our journey took us north up a hill to the beautiful town of Eyeries. Personally I'm much more used to having an engine on my bike, so having to resort to physical exertion in order to gain momentum was a bit disconcerting. The girls were obviously a lot more used to it than me, and sped on ahead. Bettina was a dab hand at it in fact and often took the lead, leaving Beatrice and me alternatively trailing in her wake. After ten kilometres of rippling hills we limped into town and took a well deserved break.

The sky had remained overcast for the duration of the journey, but was beginning to clear now. We pulled up in the centre of town by the church. The town was made up of brightly coloured houses. It wasn't very big, but that didn't stop it having three pubs. We selected one and popped in for an Irish coffee. At the rear of the pub was a large window presenting a fantastic view of the rolling rugged landscape that stretched out to Dursey Island at the very tip of the peninsula. It was also the next leg of our journey.

The next destination was Allihies. The sign read seventeen kilometres, which wouldn't have been too bad if not for the fact that ten of them were uphill. At the first hill I had the grand plan of taking a run up. I figured that if I could gain enough momentum at the bottom then it would carry me up the worst of the hill. It nearly worked. However, I had expelled all my energy on the run up and henceforth collapsed in a pathetic heap halfway, and had to walk the rest. I took solace in the knowledge that there would be a large hill to glide down on the other side. It was the only time I ever stayed ahead of the girls.

We stopped at the top of one of those hills for a breather, and to take in the magnificent view, and to rest our sore arses. What is it about bicycles? Why, with all this new technology, can they not build an efficient and more comfortable seat that doesn't leave your arse feeling like it has been swiped repeatedly with a large wooden object by a draconian headmaster? I mean, I'm sure that bicycle companies spend millions on research for improving the efficiency of their machines: weight, aerodynamics, versatility and others such technical things. They could at least think about the rider's comfort in the process. It's not too much to ask and would have improved the quality of my day.

Once rested, we glided down the biggest hill yet and through a tiny village. At the end of the village was yet another bloody hill. As I puffed my way up, with Beatrice and Bettina yet again in front of me, a woman in a passing car gave me an amused look. So much for male superiority, she must have been thinking.

We soon reached the top of the next hill and were pleased to see the road now ran along the rocky cliffs that were a sea of gentle rippling hills, easier on the legs but the side of this road did slide steeply off down to the rocky coastline below; which was a slight cause for watching where we were going. We stopped along the way and sat by the side of the road for a while. A lone seal was swimming in the surf far down below. This was a wild and quite desolate landscape. Along the way we had only seen the one small village and the occasional lone house in the middle of a giant field of vivid green grass, backed by rugged hills and cliffs amid sparkling blue inlets. Most of the houses, even the lone ones, were painted in various bright, vivid colours. In the winter it can rain here for months on end. This lovely sunny day was more than likely a rarity on this peninsula. I could see the need for colour in the lives of these people.

Once we reached Allihies, I headed straight for the nearest pub and ordered a pint of Murphy's. I needed the iron. I also hoped it would numb the pain a bit. At the end of the bar, by the window, sat an old man wearing a flat cap and nursing a small glass of stout. He eyed me curiously as I took a sip of my pint, and then suddenly blurted: 'Where yous fram?'

'England,' I answered, after wiping up the splattered beer that I had coughed over the bar top.

'Ah! And where yous goin to?'

'Dursey Island.'

'Ah!' he murmured, and then turned his attention back to his glass of stout.

I picked up my pint and took it outside. The sky was completely clear now and the sun was beating down upon us. It was a beautiful day.

Copper was discovered here in 1810 and this had fuelled the wealth of the Puxley family (who had once owned that mansion back in Castletownbere). They owned the land at the time. The last mine closed in 1962, but in its day 30,000 tonnes of copper was being exported from this region, albeit somewhat at the expense of the workforce who suffered from low wages and dangerous, unhealthy working conditions. At one time that workforce numbered 1300 men, women and children. Experienced Cornish miners were also brought in. It seemed that the many roofless stone cottages we had passed along the way had belonged to them.

Refuelled, we soldiered on. Four kilometres out of town we came across the turn off for Dursey Island. It was eight kilometres to the cable car. A sixteen-kilometre round trip, because it was the only road in and out. The girls wanted to go, or more to the point Bettina wanted to go.

'I have never seen a cable car go across the water before,' she argued.

'It's no different to any other cable car, it just goes across water,' I argued back. 'You must see cable cars all the time in Switzerland.'

'Yes, but not one that goes over water.'

It seemed Bettina was adamant about this.

As we stood there arguing, a car pulled up to the junction. We questioned the driver as to the number of hills along this road.

'Oh it's not that bad,' he replied, confidently.

You would say that, I thought, you've got a car.

I really didn't want to go any further, other than back to the hostel. It was getting to the point where I could hardly manage to sit on my seat at all. My legs felt like lead weights. The spirit was willing, but the body was just not up to it.

In the end I relented. After all, I had subjected these poor girls to the pitfalls of my personal challenge the other day, so I guess this was a sort of penance for what I had put them through.

Despite more hellish physical exertion it was worth the ride because this road took us through the most spectacular scenery yet: through small rocky valleys awash with those old roofless stone cottages, and grass that was a deep, lush green. It was six in the afternoon when we arrived at the embarkation point. The cable car closes down from six until seven. How's that for bad timing? We had no choice but to wait. The area has a small scattering of B&Bs and a restaurant. The restaurant was closed so we sat outside.

Dursey Island is a small place, just six and a half kilometres long by one and a half wide and lying just 250 metres off the tip of the peninsula. According to the guidebook around twenty people lived there, along with their cattle. I wondered why they had gone to the trouble of building a cable car when they could have just ferried them across the stretch on a boat. But then again, looking at the stretch of water between the two land masses it became clear why. The small boat attempting to navigate this was being tossed about like a branch in river rapids. The cable car is the only one in the whole of Ireland. Ironically, the cattle gets precedence over human beings during crossings. This tiny stretch of water separating the two land masses was once littered with the bodies of the three hundred people who sought refuge here in 1602 when the English attacked Dunboy Castle. They were slaughtered and thrown into the sea.

When seven came it still didn't move. This time the girls had had enough and announced that we were leaving. We had left the town and got to the top of the hill when I happened to glance back and see that the cable car was now moving. I shouted to the others and they spun around and came back for a look. I figured that as we nearly killed ourselves getting here, we might as well see what we came to see.

'How was it for you?' I asked Bettina.

'Like a cable car going over water,' she replied.

Back at the junction it was a further seventeen kilometres back to the hostel. Hans was right about there being a nice long descent to the hostel. However I was right about us having to get up to it first. That last seventeen kilometres was a sea of huge rippling hills, the worst we had come across yet. The hostel entrance, as we rounded a corner, was a sight for sore arses let me tell you.

As we revelled in the joy of making it home alive, I suddenly realised that we still had to go to town and get some food. I suggested a takeaway I had spotted the day before. There was no way in hell I was going to do any cooking tonight. Bettina and I volunteered to go. By this time my arse was so sore that I couldn't even sit on the seat, not even for a moment. I rode the entire way there and back, throbbing cheeks held high in the air. Anyone behind me might have mistaken them for the face of a drunken villager staggering home.

Back at the hostel we laid out the plates, distributed the food, laid out the cushions on the chairs and then winced as we sat down to eat.

9

Tourists and a Dolphin

The next day we took our bags and our tender cheeks on a bus back to Glengarriff. The girls then got on a bus to Killarney, as they were running short of time. Time wasn't a restriction for me. I always try to make sure of that. There is nothing worse than having to rush around a country. I always prefer to stop and smell the roses. I like to spend time in the country and soak up the atmosphere, get to know the people, how they live and what they do for fun. Besides, my legs weren't about to go anywhere after the few days I'd just had.

My intention had been to spend a quiet day in the hostel, writing my journal and reading. Alas that wasn't to be. A Dutch couple came in and the guy was an incessant talker. Before I knew it I had made a bunch of new friends and we all went out for a drink at Barry Murphy's bar that evening. That's the one thing that never ceases to amaze me about the backpacker scene: no sooner have you said goodbye to one group of friends than you find yourself befriending a new set. Amongst this group was Anne from London. Anne had given up her job in costume design and come out here to Ireland in search of something new. Although she didn't quite know what, yet.

The next morning Anne and I took the bus to Killarney. The instant we entered County Kerry the roads were awash with white tourist buses filled, in all probability, with Americans. According to the people we had spoken to along the Beara Peninsula, at this time of year they infest the area like cockroaches. Killarney is the starting point for the Ring of Kerry. As it was mid-June, that particular peninsula was crawling with tourists. This was the other reason I'd decided to explore the Beara Peninsula: it is less visited and unspoilt by its visitors. According to reports from other people, the Ring of Kerry is an area of outstanding beauty. But I decided to leave it for another day, preferably out of season.

There is more accommodation here than anywhere else, other than Dublin. So we figured we wouldn't have much trouble finding a place to stay. We got beds in the *Killarney Railway Hostel*, which was a quaint little place with names for its dorms instead of numbers. Anne and I were separated and I was put in the Porcupine Room. Judging by the large plastic panniers piled in the corner, I assumed that one of my roommates was the owner of the motorcycle I had seen parked outside. Even in the summer Ireland wasn't the best of places for touring on a motorcycle.

Killarney's streets were covered in crap (no I don't mean the tourists). Horse-drawn carriages offer a scenic tour of the city and the surrounding areas. The carriages have been in use for well over a hundred years. Explains the amount of dung along the roads. You'd have thought that after all that time they might have managed to clean some of it up. As we passed the row of horses waiting for more customers, their faces seemed to wear a look of sheer dejection; possibly due to their days being spent pulling around overweight middle-aged Americans loaded down with video cameras and ice creams.

To the south-west of the town lies the Killarney National Park, a 10,000-hectare parkland. Enclosed within the park are three beautiful lakes, a network of cycling and walking trails and all manner of sights, including an old restored castle and monastic ruins. It was quite late by the time we had settled in so we took a short walk along the fringes of this park before returning and getting ready for a night out.

Killarney is probably the only town in Ireland that obeys its licensing laws. We had spent the first couple of hours in a nice quiet pub on the edge of town, and decided to go and look for some music. We left the pub at 11.20 and found all the others were also closing. We walked around for ages trying to find at least one that was open. After much questioning we were finally directed to a large bar by a group of Irishmen. That closed shortly after, so the same guys came over and took us to Ruby's night-club.

'You won't have to pay, now,' he said. 'I'll get you in for free.'

And that he did. As we entered he told the doorman we were with him, and he waved us through. VIP treatment, I like it. For some strange reason though, they refused to serve draught beers after midnight. Two shorts cost over six pounds. I hate tourist towns!

The many smouldering turds lying in the middle of the road represented this town exactly: crap. Killarney seemed to illustrate everything that mass tourism does to destroy a place. The one thing that attracts these people to a place like this, gets ruined by the amount of people that come here over the summer months. I hoped that it wouldn't be so bad outside of the high season, but would have to wait until another day to find out. Anne and I had both agreed wholeheartedly on this, and couldn't wait to get out. We took a bus to Dingle the next day.

Dingle is the principle town on the Dingle Peninsula, just above the Ring of Kerry. It was different to the Beara Peninsula in that it was greener, smoother and lusher. The bus took us on a hair-raising ride along narrow, hilly roads, past beautiful beaches, and also past the curiously named *Bog View Hostel*. The only unattractive feature was those bloody tourist buses.

Upon arrival we stayed in *An Caladh Spainneach* (no I haven't just been sick) hostel, which actually means *The Spanish Harbour*. The more I was hearing of the Irish language, the more convinced I was becoming that it wasn't really a language at all, but more of an incoherent slur. I was just glad I didn't have to learn it. The words seemed impossible to pronounce.

Anne and I were put in separate-sex dorms. I waded into my dorm through a pile of open luggage, discarded clothes and rubbish, and dumped down my pack. It seemed I had some very messy roommates. I had the top bunk, so I clambered up and put on my bed sheets then met Anne downstairs.

Dingle's principle attraction is a dolphin, believe it or not. Back in 1984, fishermen started noticing a solitary bottlenose dolphin that seemed to have made its home in the entrance to the harbour. It used to follow the boats, jumping and playing in their wake, and even leaping over the boat on occasions.

The dolphin was named Fungie and is now an international celebrity. Down at the harbour there are many boats offering trips out to see Fungie. The trip is free if he doesn't show. Although it seems that he usually does.

Fungie can also be watched from the shore, although not as close up. Anne and I decided to do that. I figured we could watch him for longer that way. We hiked out about a mile or so, over rocks and along beaches until we came to the entrance to the harbour. We then perched ourselves on the hillside ready for Fungie to show himself. He didn't. The only thing that showed itself was the rain. As it began we climbed back up to the top and looked for shelter. We were in the middle of a field and there was no cover for miles. Fortunately Anne had an umbrella. We must have looked a pathetic sight huddled under an umbrella, cameras poised and ready to shoot. All this just to see a dolphin.

Fungie still didn't show. The wind was starting to blow up now and I for one was freezing. I spotted a disused light-house a bit further along and suggested to Anne that we go and see if we can shelter there. She agreed. Well, there wasn't any shelter. But there was a middle-aged couple standing behind the building using it as a wind break. They hadn't seen Fungie either. Eventually he showed when the boats came out. As they circled around at the harbour entrance, Fungie made brief appearances next to them, but didn't do anything spectacular. He disappeared once they left. The rain had also disappeared, so we made our way back to town.

I got my first taste of traditional Irish music here in Dingle. It soon transpired that pub music in Ireland is like nothing you've ever seen before. We passed a sign advertising a *Trad Session* at five. It was nearly that now, so we went in, ordered a couple of beers and sat down. I expected to see a stage set up, with PAs and microphones. But there was nothing. After a while, I watched as three men came in, each carrying a large black case, and seated themselves around a table by the window. One of them wandered up to the bar and ordered three pints of the Black Stuff, then returned to the table with them. After sipping their beer and chatting for a while they each brought out an instrument: a violin, banjo and accordion. They then proceeded to play. It was all very casual, and they took long breaks in-between to sip beer and gather inspiration.

After that we went for a bite to eat. Anne reminded me that it was Father's Day back home, so I figured I ought to phone home. On the way back to the hostel I popped into the takeaway to get some change for the phone. I was served by a woman with big thick glasses, who thanked me. 'My pleasure,' I replied, a little confused.

My dad seemed a bit concerned that I was spending so much time in the pub. I think he was worried I'd become an alcoholic. I told him not to worry and that I'd do my best to make sure I curb my drinking, then said goodbye and joined Anne down the pub. Here we spent the most fantastic evening listening to a two-piece band. The female singer had the most amazingly powerful yet dulcet voice.

Anne left the next day for Doolin. During our trip Anne and I had been discussing the Fridge Book. In this book the author describes his discovery of a King in Ireland. It appears that on Tory Island, just off the northern coast of County Donegal, lives Patsy Dan Rodgers. As a bit of a joke Patsy had been dubbed King of Tory – a perfect example of the Irish people's sense of humour – his role being to promote the island and attract visitors. However the name has stuck and he is known all over Ireland by this title. Anne and I decided it would be fun to go to a remote island and visit a King. So we made arrangements to meet up again in Galway and head up from there. She gave me the number of her mobile phone (posh traveller) and I agreed to phone her when I got there.

I wanted to stay another day to see if I could get a better look at Fungie. I also decided to change hostels. On the outskirts of town was the extremely popular *Rainbow Hostel*. Aside from the fact that I was curious to see what it was like, the tiny shower in the one where I was staying served as an added incentive to get out of this one. There was hardly enough room to swing a Leprechaun. The guidebook said that the Rainbow Hostel was 300 metres west of town, so I decided to walk it. After all, I was a real backpacker now.

It soon turned out to be a damn sight more than 300 metres. However, the move was a good one. I got a bed in a huge dorm all to myself. There was no bunk bed above it, and it was right by the window. The window presented a view of rolling green fields along with the sounds of the country. I just hoped those sounds didn't wake up too early in the morning.

Once I'd settled in I wandered back out to the harbour entrance again to see if Fungie would be more active today. Again I waited and waited and he only appeared when the boats came. I was beginning to suspect a conspiracy here. If I'd had more time I would have investigated further. I suspected that the real Fungie had actually died of old age and the tourist board, obviously realising that with their main attraction gone tourism could well die in this town, had developed and built a mechanical dolphin. This dolphin is equipped with a high-tech computer system that is programmed to respond to a signal sent from the tourist boats.

So whenever they come out, so does he. With that thought, I wandered back to town, popped into the *Marina Inn*, got myself a pint and added another stain to my collection.

The secret of Dingle's tourist trade?

*

The hostel was situated in an old farmhouse. It was a very peaceful area. The only downside was the lack of facilities in the kitchen. At breakfast the next morning the kettle, which had worked the previous day, seemed not to today. I had to pilfer some water boiled in a saucepan by another guest.

As I sat down and drank my coffee I was greeted by the guy sitting opposite. He recognised me from the hostel in Killarney. I had recognised his motorbike outside, but not him, as I hadn't actually seen him in Killarney, just his luggage. He was from Germany and was spending two and half weeks here in Ireland on the bike. Although, as I had guessed, he was finding it bad weather for motorcycling.

For over a week now it had been raining in the morning. Today was no exception. The hostel ran a shuttle bus into town, so I enquired at reception about getting on it. The next was at 9.45. I had ten minutes. I put my bag in the van and waited. I kept a watchful eye on the bus whilst listening to a couple of guys sitting nearby discussing the politics of their countries: Canada and France. They also talked about the abortion debate and how a doctor was shot and killed outside a hospital by a protestor. The other pointed out the irony that someone who is protesting about the so-called murder of human life, could then go and take one themselves. A good point.

The driver finally emerged at 10.15 and walked straight past me to the van. The girl told me to follow him. Before I had even shut the door he started to drive off. My 'hello' was greeted with silence. As we squeezed past a broken down truck further down the road, I tried once again to engage him in conversation. No reply. He just stopped the van, got out and wandered over. He didn't seem to give a shit that I had a bus to catch. Shortly after he returned and continued driving.

At the bus stop he just managed to utter the words, 'That's your bus.' I thanked him, not knowing why I should, and dashed through the driving rain to the waiting bus. As I found my seat a couple came on and reluctantly had to sit apart. I would have swapped seats and let them be together, but I wanted the window seat. So I remained where I was. The girl sat next to me and the guy shot me a hard look, as if to say: 'Don't even think about it, mate!' I hadn't, and didn't have any intention of it by the look of her. Instead I put on my headphones and whiled away the time listening to the sweet voice of Mariah Carey.

I took the bus to Tralee. Upon arrival I headed into town. At *Finnegan's Hostel* I banged on the huge door. Strangely, it seemed to open of its own accord. I looked downwards to see a little girl's head poking out from behind. Her smiling face took on a frightened look when I asked for a dorm bed.

'Oh that's my daughter, she doesn't work here,' came a woman's voice from the top of the stairs, who then proceeded to show me to reception.

I was checked in by a girl from England. She explained that she had been living and working here in Tralee for the past ten years.

'I love it here,' she said. 'It's so much nicer than England. The people aren't in so much of a rush, and things are a lot cheaper. It costs me a lot less to run my car over here.'

I agreed with her on many things, except about things being cheaper. One thing Ireland isn't, and that's cheap. Food was quite expensive. Beer was cheap if it was stout, but outside that it was actually quite expensive. And VAT was higher.

With all the rain I seemed to be heading into, I figured it was time I bought myself a raincoat. After all, there was only so much time before my luck ran out. So I wandered into town.

Tralee looked to be a nice little town. It would look a lot nicer when all the roadworks are finished in the town centre. I wandered into Dunnes Store and once I had acquired a raincoat, I went for my customary afternoon pint and beer stain collection in a little place called *The Rambling House*, and then took a walk to the Blennerville Windmill just outside town.

Blennerville used to be the chief port of Tralee. However, it has long since silted up. A flour mill was built here in 1800 but fell into disuse in 1880. It has now been restored and is the largest working mill in Ireland. It was from here that thousands of immigrants boarded so-called 'coffin ships' for a new life in the USA. One of those ships was the *Jeannie Johnston* which ferried thousands of immigrants to Baltimore, New York and Quebec back in the 1800s without ever losing a single passenger to disease. Quite an achievement, back then. Out the back of the flour mill's Visitor Centre an exact replica of that ship was being built. It looked magnificent, but I wondered if it was a bit extravagant to spend thousands of pounds restoring an old ship that would just sit in a harbour for tourists to be photographed on.

As I wandered back to town I was greeted by passers-by and waved at by people passing in their cars. It takes a bit of getting used to, this friendliness towards strangers.

I passed by Paddy Mac's pub in town and noticed a sign advertising traditional Irish music at nine that night. So I returned after having eaten a cremated pizza for dinner. Somehow I never seem to get that right. It's the simplest of things to cook, you just shove it in the oven for fifteen minutes and it's done. But I always seem to forget about them.

As I entered the pub it was quarter to nine. Once again there was no band setting up. In fact the place was virtually empty. The whole place was made of old, dark-stained wood: the floor, the bar and all the tables. A couple of Americans were sitting by the door, obviously waiting too. I wandered up to the bar and ordered a pint of Guinness. 'Is there any music tonight?' I asked.

'Ah sure, dey'll be in around nine-tirty,' replied the barman.

So I took my pint and sat down by the window. Half an hour later two men came in carrying the familiar black boxes and sat down next to me. After ordering their pints they greeted me and then pulled out their instruments and begun playing. Once again I was astounded by just how casual this all was. These people had sat next to me, just as though they were having a pint.

A quarter of the way into the session the door opened and in walked a fella carrying a guitar. He came over and asked the two playing if he could join in. To my surprise they agreed, quite happily. So he sat down and the three of them played together. It was fantastic: songs were sung, instrumentals were played and much fun was had by all. These people seemed to have so much passion for their music, even though they didn't really have much of an audience. Aside from myself, the few Americans and a small family that had come in later, the place was pretty much empty. They didn't seem to care, though. They just loved to play their music, regardless of how many people were listening. I just loved that. The only thing missing was the Sisters of Murphy's. I was looking forward to influencing and coaxing them with my fair words, and had been placing my pint precariously on the edge of the table, yet still they hadn't shown.

Back at the hostel I spent a very restless night being constantly woken by an old man in my dorm who kept getting up periodically through the night to take a piss and fart loudly in the bathroom. Normally having an en-suite toilet is a luxury in a hostel. But not this night.

___10___

An Odd Blend of Music

Doolin is a small village in County Clare that is reputed to have some of the best music pubs in the west of Ireland. It is also the embarkation point for the ferry to the smallest of the Aran Islands, Inisheer. This was my main reason for wanting to go there.

Along the way the bus made a surprise stop at the Cliffs of Moher, reputed to be one of the most spectacular sights in Ireland. We had crossed the River Shannon and were now in County Clare. The driver informed us that we had one hour to spend here, before they continued on to Doolin. This was unplanned. Great! Doolin was only ten kilometres up the road so I wondered if maybe I should walk it. But I figured that one mammoth hike with my backpack was enough for one journey. Instead I left it on the bus and went to explore the area.

The Cliffs of Moher are made up of soft shale and sandstone. They are so unstable that even the birds don't nest there. The highest point is 203 metres. Being on the West

Coast, I imagined that the sunsets would be magnificent. Unfortunately that was a long way off, so I contented myself with looking over the edge. The best way to do this, it seemed, was to lie down flat on your front and slither up to it. Everybody else was doing it. One section of the cliffs had been strengthened specifically for this purpose.

A solid concrete patio had been built on the cliff edge. Finding a free spot at the edge wasn't a problem, as it seemed that not many people were willing to risk their lives for this spectacle. I lay my camera by my side and assumed the position. Very slowly, I crawled my way forward until my eyes peered over the edge. The cliff dropped off at ninety degrees to the sight and booming sound of tiny jagged rocks being pounded by the waves far below. It was also the weirdest feeling. Your whole body seems to go numb and all sorts of crazy thoughts enter your head. Although you know that you are perfectly safe because you are lying on flat ground, you still imagine that you are about to fall off because your head goes all dizzy, and you start to push back for fear of sliding off the edge. It's quite an eerie sensation

In the distance I could see the outline of the Aran Islands, almost as though they were an oil painting on the horizon. To the north the rocky coastline ran off into the distant haze to what was apparently Galway Bay and the hills of the Connemara. The cliffs stretch for eight kilometres from Hags Head in the south right up to Doolin. From Doolin up to Galway lies an area called the Burren, which is a landscape 160 square kilometres in size comprising solely of limestone rock. The Burren is a wilderness, flat and sloping and broken by great hillsides of limestone separated by cliffs like giant steps. The area is also rich in archaeological sites.

It's possible to walk the entire length of the Cliffs of

Moher, part of which was walled off by an eccentric landlord back in the 1800s. I wandered along here and then onwards for a while. Then I decided to sit on the edge. Even here the cliffs still represented a sheer vertical drop down onto the jagged rocks far below. It's a magnificent yet fearful view, especially as the birds are flying around in the distance below you. Yet somehow it's hard to resist stepping as close to the edge as you possibly can. I wondered how many people had taken that one step too far.

The last few miles to Doolin took us through tiny, narrow country roads, hemmed in by the familiar sight of stone walls, like the one I had fallen on back in Baltimore. Our driver didn't seem to care about the narrowness of the roads and zoomed along them like a truck driver on speed. He screeched to a halt directly opposite *Paddy's Hostel*, which was just where I had intended to stay.

I was checked in at reception by Danny, a very chirpy Irishman. Danny was happy because he was on holiday as of tomorrow. It appeared that Doolin, like Adrigole, was just an area and not a town. It stretched several kilometres along the coast. Apparently I was in, what was known as, the Lower Village. There wasn't much: one shop, a few restaurants and pubs. My main reason for coming here was to get a ferry out to Inisheer. It was too late to go over now, so I got the required information and then relaxed a bit before going to the pub.

Doolin is extremely popular with backpackers and music lovers. Apparently it attracts a very eclectic crowd. This was quite evident in the pub that night. I was sitting by the bar listening to some very good traditional Irish folk music, when all of a sudden I heard, what sounded like a Digeridoo. At first I thought I was hearing things, but further investigation proved it to be very real indeed. The guy playing was incredible, and somehow blended his Australian music perfectly with the Irish music. During the day Doolin had been very quiet. But now it seemed that the people crawled out of the woodwork and headed for the pubs at night. So once again I found myself knocking back the Irish stout and enjoying the wonderful atmosphere of the Craic.

__11__

__Man of Aran__

When I got to the terminal the following morning I discovered that the ferry was fully booked. The next one was over an hour away. As I waited I was joined by Peggy and Margaret from Australia. Margaret had just come to see Peggy off. She told me that we had already met.

'Really!' I said. 'Where?'

'At the lighthouse in Dingle. I was with an American guy and we stopped and talked to you and that girl.'

I then remembered her. The backpacker's world is a small place. I also seemed to have the impression that I knew Peggy from somewhere. Her voice sounded familiar. It turned out that she had been in Anne's dorm back in Dingle. I had heard her talking to Anne, but hadn't seen her.

When Margaret left I chatted with Peggy while we waited for the boat to arrive. 'So what brought you to Ireland?' I asked.

'I came here last year for a short holiday and fell in love with the place. On the plane back to Oz I cried. I was so unbelievably sad to be leaving. I couldn't explain it, but I just couldn't get the country out of my mind. So I decided to come back here for a few months and see if I could get it out of my system. If not, then I don't know what I'll do next.'

This was becoming a common story.

Inisheer is just eight kilometres from Doolin. It is also the smallest of the three Aran Islands. I had bought a ticket that covered passage to all three islands and then on to Galway, at a cost of £20. My intention was to spend one night on Inisheer and then go to Inishmaan. Inishmór is the largest of the three islands, and also the most visited. For those reasons alone, I had no real interest in visiting that, especially at this time of year. Inishmaan was the least visited with just a few B&Bs and no hostel. Inisheer did have a hostel, so I decided I would stay there.

The ferry docked at the only village on the entire island, where its 300 inhabitants all live. Most of Inisheer's sights lie here in the village. The island is so small that I circumnavigated it in three hours. Peggy had elected to remain behind and lay on the beach, as it was a gorgeous day. Once I left the village I found myself looking across a flat, treeless terrain, the whole of which had been sectioned off into grids by stone walls. Again none of these walls were cemented. Each stone was carefully laid in place. The entire island, it seemed, was just one big wall. A nasty thought popped into my head. What if I were to kick the corner of one those walls, would it create a domino effect over the whole island? It was an interesting thought. However, I didn't fancy a bunch of irate locals after me. On an island this size there wasn't much chance of remaining hidden for long. There was a timelessness about the place and I didn't want to end up stoned to death or hung by a lynch mob.

Since leaving the village I hadn't seen a soul. All I saw were some sheep and a few goats. The beach near the pier was the only one; the rest of the coastline was rocky. These islands are made from the same stretch of limestone as the Burren on the mainland, which stretches out into Galway Bay and surfaces here. It was easy to see where they had got the material to build those walls. The coastline was littered with loose, broken rock, scattered everywhere. I wandered on down the eastern side, past the rusting wreck of a freighter called the *Plassy*, which was wrecked there in 1960 and thrown high up onto the rocks. The islanders rescued the crew from the vessel during storm force weather without the loss of a single sailor. It was in later years that the strong waves from the Atlantic Ocean threw the wreck upon the rocks well above the high tide mark. This wreck is the one in the opening credits of the TV comedy *Father Ted*, in case you're interested.

I carried on to the lighthouse lying at the southern half of the island. Again I had seen nobody, just cows, sheep and goats. The sky was perfectly clear and to all intents and purposes I could well have been on an island in Greece, not off the coast of rainy Ireland.

Whilst wandering along the southern half, I hit upon an idea. I remembered hearing a story about a man who had put a note in a bottle, saying that whomever finds it is invited to write him a letter, and had launched it from the southern shores of the UK. Years later he received a letter from a woman in Australia who had found his message in a bottle and decided to write and let him know. I wasn't sure how true it was, but it was an interesting concept. As I stared out westward, I realised there were thousands of miles of tumultuous ocean out there, and a corked bottle could end up pretty much anywhere, having been dragged by surface currents and winds. No matter how ferocious the storm or high the waves, the bottle would never sink and would therefore continue drifting until it eventually hit land.

I decided I wanted to send one, a millennium message in a bottle. But instead of leaving an address and phone number, I would leave an e-mail address. After all, this is the technical age, and I do keep moving about so much these days. Later that day I wrote my message, found an adequately sized bottle and planned to launch it the next day.

Back at the hostel, I joined Peggy and we relaxed on the wall outside. It really was the most gorgeous day. The sun was shining and the sea was sparkling blue, almost Mediterranean-like. This island exuded a very peaceful atmosphere indeed. The only sound to be heard was that of a tiny radio somewhere in the distance playing Irish folk music.

Right next door to the hostel was a pub. Very handy, I thought. Danny, it seemed, had taken his holiday over here. We found him sitting outside the pub. He explained that he would be playing guitar in the pub that night. So after watching the sunset, Peggy and I wandered in, ordered a beer each and found a couple of seats in the corner. Danny came in shortly after and proceeded to play a few sets of Irish music. Instead of payment for his performance though, he was being supplied with free beer all night, as much as he could drink; which was quite a lot, it seemed. This appeared to be a common custom for many of the smaller pubs around Ireland. A beneficial deal for both parties I suppose, depending on how much the musician likes to drink.

As the evening progressed more people came in. When

the official closing time came they just pulled down the blinds. There isn't a single policeman on any of these islands, so you wouldn't think late closing would present a problem. Well it hadn't, until one day. Robert, who had come over from the mainland to study at the Irish language school here, told me what had happened. The mainland Gardaí sent one of their men to Inisheer disguised as a backpacker. The result was the three pubs on the island being charged and fined for serving out of hours. All night to be exact. Well, with no police there was no need to shut, was there? Nowadays it seems they still don't shut on time, they are just more alert to outsiders.

Instead of showing remorse or embarrassment for what happened though, the people of the island decided to immortalise this event by proudly framing a newspaper article and displaying it on the wall of their pub. The headline read:

THE LANDLORD THAT TIME FORGOT.

Next to this was an artist's impression of the event. The drawing was of a pub with its blinds down and showed the image of people partying inside, along with a few drunks stumbling around or passed out against rocks outside. Figures wearing backpacks were hiding behind walls and sneaking along the roof. The caption read:

Everyone knows there are no police on Inisheer.

The whole thing seemed to epitomise the ideal that the Irish people live by. If you can't beat them, then have a laugh about it.

I found this hysterical. I looked at Peggy's watch and saw

that it was well past midnight. I had no idea where the time had gone. I was about to light a cigarette when I suddenly heard the most angelic voice coming from behind me. Instantly intrigued I wandered over, cigarette in mouth and match ready to strike. Sitting around a table was a group of local girls, of various ages. One of the girls was singing a song. Her eyes were closed and she sang this song with a passion that came straight from the heart. The lack of music seemed not to make the slightest difference to her rendition of this song.

Never before had I heard such a sweet and beautiful voice. Everybody in the room had shut up, and all eyes and ears were focused on this girl's moment. The entire room was deathly silent. You could have heard an ant fart. You could also have heard a match being struck. Instinctively I knew that even the sound of a striking match would be completely disrespectful and spoil this girl's moment. So I put the match and cigarette away and joined everyone else as they basked in this wonderful atmosphere. The entire pub had given this girl centre stage. When she finished, the girl next to her sang her song, and so on. Each time the people in the pub gave these girls their undivided attention. I couldn't imagine that happening back home. People would continue talking and probably tell her to shut up. But singing, it seemed, has a special place in the hearts of the Irish people, and each singer deserves to be heard. I was completely bowled over by just how wonderful these girls' voices were. I fell in love many times over that night, and vowed to marry each one of those girls (if they ever legalise polygamy) and start my own harem of female Irish singers, led by Andrea Corr of course.

*

In the morning I showered, dressed and walked outside to sample the beautiful day. The instant I stepped out the door I was overcome with how quiet it was. I checked the time. It was gone ten o'clock. It seemed more like six. The island was bathed in a tranquil silence. It was almost like stepping into a void, or as if I had suddenly been rendered completely deaf. It was actually noisier indoors than it was outside. I decided there and then that I was going to stay another day. This is an atmosphere that should be savoured. I also thought it such a pity that most people only spend a few hours on the island and then go back to the mainland. They are missing so much. Upon arrival yesterday Peggy and I had got talking to an American couple.

'Yeah, you know we came over intending to spend the night, but we're gonna catch the next boat back,' said the guy. 'We're pretty much done with the island now.'

In other words they'd had a quick look around and now think that they know everything about it. I thought it such a shame that they would go away with absolutely no knowledge of Inisheer, other than the fact that it looks pretty.

The hostel wasn't busy. Apart from a few teenage girls from the mainland, the only other guests were a couple of Scandinavian girls. However, that was to change. Today was Friday, and the hostel was to fill up.

That afternoon I returned to the southern part of the island with the intention of launching my millennium message in a bottle. The sky was once again completely clear, but away from the village the wind was quite fierce, resulting in many unsuccessful launches. The only bottle I could find was an empty plastic mineral water bottle, so it proved impossible against the wind. Each launch was caught by a gust of wind that blew it further back inland, and I had to walk back and retrieve it. When I did manage to get it out into the water the tide just brought it right the way back again. So I gave up and returned to the hostel.

It seemed that mainlanders came over here to party at the weekends. When I returned from a walk I found Peggy talking to one of them. Lesley was from County Wexford and had come here on holiday with her younger sister and her friend Caroline. Lesley had been here a few times before and absolutely loved the place. I could understand that. Later that night we all went out to one of the other pubs in the town. As the evening progressed the place became completely packed out. Four men sat in the corner playing traditional music all night.

Robert turned up with a friend from the language school. They explained to me that this is one of the best places to come to if you want to learn Irish. Gaelic is the island's first language. During my stay I had heard the islanders using it in everyday conversation. They only really used English when needed, and switched between the two with considerable ease. Robert explained that in the Irish school no English is allowed to be spoken. If you spoke so much as one sentence whilst in class, then you were expelled from the school and sent home. Sounds a bit harsh, I thought. But Robert didn't seem to think so. 'It's the best way to discipline you into speaking the language,' he explained. 'Otherwise it would be too easy to just resort to English when you get stuck.'

It turned out to be a good night, except for one incident. I was standing at the end of the bar trying to get another drink. It was gone two in the morning and the bar seemed to be shut. However, people were still partying. There was no one behind the bar so I waited for someone to come back, in the hope of managing to convince him to pour me another pint. (See what this country is doing to me.) As I stood there a fella about my age came over and started talking to me. He was so drunk he could hardly stand up. He was friendly enough though, and we chatted for about ten minutes. Shortly after he went away, one of his friends came over. He was a giant of a man with a shaved head, muscles the size of my neck and an intimidating look about him.

'What were you saying to him?' he growled.

'We were just having a chat,' I replied, gulping. I had no idea what his problem was, and to be honest didn't really want to find out. I just wanted another pint, not a fight. And I certainly didn't want a fight with this fella. I doubted I would last five minutes. Somehow I could see all of this wonderful night crumbling down before me. I'd been having such a good time and all, enjoying the music and Craic of Ireland. Up until this point I'd hardly believed there could be arseholes like this around. But sadly, just like any other country, Ireland has its share.

Fortunately the other guy returned and somehow pacified him, and he went away. What the hell was all that about? I wondered, as I walked back to the others.

I never did get another pint, so I left the pub alone and wandered back to the hostel. Down the end of the street I noticed my drunken friend collapsed against a wall. His two friends were shouting at him to get up. The giant was especially annoyed. I decided to take a different route, not wanting another confrontation.

Once safely tucked up in bed, I was just about to drop off to sleep when the door suddenly burst open and, to my immense horror, the same two guys came in dragging their drunken friend behind them and proceeded to dump him on the bed next to mine. They then came in and out of the room and ran around the hostel making loads of noise. The hostel owners lived in the adjacent house, so they never heard anything. It took me ages to get to sleep.

They left the next morning. It appeared they had wreaked havoc in the hostel during the night, going in and out of the dorms making lots of noise and, for some inexplicable reason, leaving fire extinguishers there. The weather had also taken a turn for the worse. The sun was now hidden behind a thick cloud of rain. Peggy and I were leaving today anyway. Peggy was going to Inishmór and spending the night there. I was heading to Galway. I'd like to have stayed longer, but I had a King to meet. Now it's not every day you can write that in a book, especially about Ireland.

In order to get to Galway, I had to take the ferry to Inishmór and then get on another. The rain had stopped by the time we arrived at Inishmór. I had an hour to kill before my ferry left and so I walked into town with Peggy. She had booked a hostel, but it was two kilometres out of town. She tried one in town, but they were fully booked. The island was holding some kind of boat race and the streets were swarming with people. Needless to say accommodation was hard to come by.

Inishmór is 14.5 kilometres long and four kilometres at its widest point. With a whopping 800 inhabitants it also has the largest population.

The ferry was half an hour late getting in. It also took longer than scheduled to get to Galway; Irish punctuality, I suppose. However, after the experience with the bus back in Adrigole I had started arriving earlier than usual. I passed the journey talking to Eleanor from Dublin. She also helped me to perform the launch of my millennium message in a bottle. I wondered where it would end up and if anyone would ever find it. But knowing my luck, it would probably wash back up on the shores of Inisheer and become a good snack for a hungry goat.

It turned out that there was a Kinlay House hostel in Galway too. I opted to stay there, as the one in Cork had been really nice. I said goodbye to Eleanor and promised to look out for her in a couple of pubs that night.

The ferry docked in Galway harbour, so thankfully I didn't have a long trek into town. In actual fact the town centre was literally just around the corner. Galway turned out to be a delightfully attractive city. Its streets were narrow with old stone and wooden shopfronts. It's also one of Europe's fastest growing cities and is the fourth largest in Ireland. There's plenty of accommodation too, so I assumed that I would have no problem getting in at Kinlay House, especially as it has 150 rooms.

Kinlay House was in a large building and you had to take a lift up to it. In the lift, I befriended Ana from Spain. She was working in Dublin as an au pair, and had come here for the weekend. She told me she had seen me on the boat over. Ana was supposed to go back to Dublin that day, but as the ferry was late she had missed her bus. We both just managed to get in to the hostel. The person after me was told that they were now fully booked. It seemed that I had taken the last bed. How's that for good timing? Galway, it seemed, is a popular place.

Ana and I dumped down our packs and headed out for a bite to eat, and then went to sample the nightlife. Galway has a reputation for its lively and bohemian nightlife. The city apparently attracts musicians and artists from all over. It is also a major Gaelic centre and Irish is widely understood. This must be the largest Irish-speaking town. Drink and talk flow rapidly here, according to the guidebook.

Ana and I entered the first pub and soon found ourselves squashed among a crowd of people who were trying their best to be lively, without knocking over the person next to them. Through the gaps in the concourse of large sweaty bodies I was able to make out the hazy image of an actual bar with a row of half-filled pints of stout lining the bar top. Ana was standing behind me looking flustered after having had even more difficulty squeezing through the crowd, on account of having brought her daypack with her. Why she felt she needed to bring this with her, I didn't know. And quite frankly didn't feel it was my place to ask. Instead, I asked her if she wanted to go somewhere a little quieter. She nodded eagerly in agreement, and so once again we slogged our way through the crowd and emerged into the coolness of the fresh evening air. This was a far cry from the casual, relaxed pub atmosphere I was growing to love in this country.

We tried many more of the pubs lining the High Street and found each one equally full. I couldn't remember the names of the two pubs Eleanor had told me she was going to, and to be honest there would have been no hope of finding her in them anyway. Finally we settled on one where we were afforded the luxury of actually being able to get to the bar and order drinks. We then found a space where we could stand and talk, and suppress our annoyance each time someone bumped our drinks. Even in these precarious circumstances I still wasn't saved by the Sister's of Murphy's. I was beginning to think they didn't really exist.

__12__

<u>A Familiar Face</u>

I had to phone Anne. I wondered where she was. But the first thing on the agenda was breakfast. The groaning sounds emitting from my empty stomach wouldn't allow me to think of anything else until they were stopped. So I decided to get something in town before phoning her.

Walking down the street I spotted a familiar figure huddled against a shop window speaking on a mobile phone. It was Anne. How's that for fate? I let her finish her call and then surprised her when she turned around. She had already booked the two o'clock bus to Sligo that day, so we spent the rest of the time together. We made arrangements to connect buses at Sligo and head on to Donegal Town from there. From Donegal Town we would start our journey to Tory Island.

When I had left the hostel that morning I thought the guy on reception had looked familiar. All afternoon I couldn't get it out of my head. Where had I seen him before? Later on as I queued at reception to pay for the use of the laundry, I studied him and racked my brains as to where I knew him from. It wasn't in Ireland, so I thought back to previous trips. Toronto came to mind. The year before I had spent a week at the Global Village Backpackers in Toronto. I felt sure that was it. When I got to the front I questioned him: 'Hey, were you in a Toronto hostel last year?'

'Yes I was, how did you know?'

I was right. Dave was the one working at the hostel, and was also the guy who had helped me set up my e-mail account. After Toronto he had come over here, and had been working at Kinlay House now for around eight months.

'I'm becoming a hostel slut,' as he so eloquently put it.

That night I befriended a group from the dorm and we all went out with the intention of getting a drink. However, we didn't get moving until eleven because we had been talking so much. Thus each pub we tried had stopped serving. It was Sunday, but I had expected them to be a bit more flexible. It seemed that the bigger the town, the more they adhere to the licensing laws - or just wouldn't allow anyone in after hours. From what I could see at the entrance there was still a good crowd of drinkers inside many of the pubs. We wandered around the streets for ages in the hope of finding one pub that would at least serve one drink. Even after the others had given up I still kept on looking - how's that for desperate? It seemed I was becoming an alcoholic just like my dad feared.

But alas not a single pub would relent and allow me in for one pint. There were still plenty of people inside these pubs, but they refused to let us in. This was one of the many things I was coming to love about Ireland: long drinking up times. Back home the bell rings for last orders and you have ten minutes drinking up time. Ten minutes is really not enough time to sink a pint, without finding yourself realising, upon stepping out into the fresh night air, that gravity really does exist. But here in Ireland there was no set limit on the drinking up time. Even in places that close and stop serving at the allotted time, they still allow you to spend half an hour or even an hour to finish your drink. I liked that.

So I returned to the hostel and went to bed. I was woken in the night by the sound of a fire alarm. The high pitched ringing jarred my brain into action, but not my body. This just plainly refused to budge. I didn't need this, I had an early bus to catch. I lay in bed hoping it was a false alarm. But it kept ringing. The others in the room were obviously thinking the same, but after a while slowly and reluctantly they began to stir. Then the announcement came:

'I'm sorry ladies and gentlemen, it is a false alarm.'

Thank god. I can go back to sleep now. But that was not to be. The alarm had woken everyone in the hostel and they now felt that they all needed to go to the toilet. For the next half an hour I was kept awake by the sound of creaking doors and people running up and down the hallway.

At breakfast the next morning I chatted to two elderly New Zealand ladies who were travelling around Ireland together. They were just taking local buses and finding accommodation when they arrived at their destination. I like meeting people like that because it restores my belief that you can still be adventurous, even in old age. Most people their age would prefer to just have everything prearranged for them. And who can blame them? It's much easier, and at their age I'm sure it's no fun traipsing around looking for a place to stay. It's not much fun at my age. But it's the freedom of it that matters. I would much rather have the choice where I stay and for how long when I get there. After all, you don't know what the place is like until you are there.

I met Anne in Sligo and we continued northward to Donegal Town. However, en-route we changed our minds. We had been studying the map and deduced that it would be better to continue on to Letterkenny, as it would get us closer to Bunbeg, where the ferry leaves from. We were stowaways. But as Anne pointed out, only I was. She had a bus pass and therefore, technically, had paid for her part of the trip. I had only paid until Donegal. At Letterkenny I casually shuffled my way down and out of the bus, half expecting the driver to drag me back by the collar wanting to know why I didn't get off back in Donegal. But he didn't. Maybe I should use that scam more often.

It started to rain when we got off the bus, so we dashed into the shelter of the station's waiting room. We had covered quite a distance. Letterkenny is close to the border of Northern Ireland. It seems funny to say that because in a sense we were in Northern Ireland. The accent was distinctly more northern, that was for sure. It sounded great. The people here were every bit as nice as the ones down south.

Sitting in the corner were two old men locked in deep conversation. Standing by the door was a couple with a young child in a pushchair. I asked the woman directions to the hostel. After a lengthy discussion they offered to take us there themselves. It seemed they too were just sheltering from the rain. At this point the two old boys piped up and asked if we knew when the next bus to Derry was.

'You've missed it,' I told them. 'The bus we just got off went on to Derry.'

It seemed they had been so busy talking they missed it. They were supposed to be going to a wedding that day.

Fortunately for them, there was another bus later on. I just hoped they wouldn't miss that too.

The kindness of people never ceases to amaze me sometimes. This couple not only went out of their way to take us to the hostel, the man also dragged Anne's bag all the way there. I asked him if he wanted to take mine, but he refused. The woman didn't offer either. So maybe they weren't so nice after all.

An Australian lady ran the hostel. She informed us that it would be better to get the ferry from Magheroarty. There was a daily service at five o'clock and a local bus from here to there at one. Bus Éireann doesn't run a service beyond this part of Ireland. Between Donegal Town and here is its only route. Any further north is served by local bus and private companies. My plan had been to hitch, as I had been told by someone way back that it was easier than getting around by bus. Well not in our experience it wasn't, as it soon turned out.

__13__

An Audience With a King

I wanted to get an early start. Unfortunately Anne couldn't seem to drag herself out of bed. We left at eleven, hiked to the outskirts of town and found a suitable spot for hitching.

An hour passed and still no one had stopped. One old man did, but seemed to change his mind when he saw our bags and said that he was turning off just up the road. We had just about given up on the idea when a white van skidded to a halt. Instantly I ran over, flung open the door and stared into the face of a bloke with rotten teeth and soiled clothing.

'I can take yous as far as Kilmacrenen,' he said.

I hesitated, partly out of a slight fear of this man, but also because it wasn't very far.

He went on to say that we would have no chance of getting picked up here and would have more chance in Kilmacrenen. He was right on the first part.

We never did get this man's name, but we did learn that he was a film's location manager. It turned out that he not only knew the place in London where Anne had recently

115

worked, but had also punched out her boss. This pleased Anne immensely, as she and many others didn't like him. According to Anne, he probably deserved it.

He dropped us both off at what he considered to be a suitable spot for hitching. But it was far from suitable. Again we had no luck. What cars did pass didn't stop. To add to this it also started raining. We were now stuck in a tiny village. Many of the passing cars would indicate that they were turning off up the road. The driver would apologetically make this gesture with his hand.

'How do you know that I don't want to go that way?' I shouted at them, as they drove past and threw water my way.

I soon became aware that this probably wasn't helping our chances much of being picked up. Anyone driving behind them would no doubt become quite fearful of a rain-soaked man shouting and waving his arms frantically at the passing cars. And I suspected a few of the villagers would soon be unlocking their gun cabinets, just in case.

There and then I made a promise to myself: if I ever pass a hitch hiker in the rain I will stop and pick him up. It was a promise I knew I would never keep, mostly because I don't have a car. In a sense I didn't blame them. Two people with two big bags and a desperate look in their eyes would be enough to arouse anyone's anxieties. When the bus came through we admitted defeat and got on that.

The doors opened and Anne hoisted on her bag, waffled something to the driver and announced that she had paid for us both. She then proceeded to manoeuvre the bag down the narrow aisle. Apart from a few elderly people sitting at the front, the bus was virtually empty. Now I faced a dilemma: I had to get past these people and to an empty seat. From past experiences, I knew that the tent strapped to the bottom of my pack wouldn't fit down the aisle. The bus had already started to move. So in a flash of inspiration – mostly brought on by panic – I bent forward, hoisted up the bottom of the pack and steamed ahead. Heads moved speedily towards the windows to avoid being jabbed in the eye by the tent poles, the nun sitting a few rows back clutching onto her cross as I passed. Once safely seated I then asked Anne where the bus was going to.

'I don't know,' she replied. 'I just told him where we were heading and he charged me for it.'

The bus was chugging its way down a narrow country lane. I had absolutely no idea where we were. I poked my head through the gap between the two headrests in front and greeted the old lady sitting there: 'Hi there, where does this bus go?'

She uttered a name that was totally incomprehensible to me.

'Err, we are trying to get to Magheroarty,' I said.

'Ah! Then yous had best get off at Gortahork. From there yous can get a taxi.'

'Could we hitch?' I asked.

'Ah, I suppose so.'

Then the old lady in the adjacent seat lent across and said, 'Maybe they can get off at the turning.'

This sparked a debate between the two ladies and they took it upon themselves to work out a plan for us. For the next five minutes the bus came alive as the passengers discussed the best possible way for us to get to our destination. Then the two ladies took their suggestions to the driver. They returned saying that the driver had agreed to stop at the turn off. From there it was only two and a half miles to the ferry. With that sorted the bus then returned to silence.

We got off at the turn off and after ten minutes of unsuccessful hitching Anne suggested that we walk it. A brave suggestion on her part; these bumpy country roads played havoc with her trolley bag. Around the corner we came across the *Celtic Tavern* and decided to take a break there. I could also mark this momentous occasion with a stain in the book. Thankfully Anne had found this whole idea of collecting beer stains in the book quite amusing, and so wouldn't entertain ideas of ditching me while I went to the toilet and carrying on alone.

As we entered we found the barman sitting with his feet up watching the football. We were the only customers, until two funny old men joined us. We spent a bit too long in this pub – an easy thing to do in Ireland – and soon found that time was running short.

Back out on the road we increased our pace. We must have looked quite the odd couple: Anne was dressed in a posh leather jacket and trousers and pulled along a trolley bag, while I trudged alongside dressed in tatty jeans and jumper with an equally tatty backpack strapped to my shoulders.

I attempted to hitch as we walked. The only lift we got though, was from another white van. Katrina explained that she couldn't take us too far because she would get into trouble if she was caught. She was on her way to pick up children from the nearby school.

'That's fine,' I said. 'Just take us as far as you can.'

And that she did. About 500 metres up the hill, in fact. Around the corner was a small village and everyone there knew her. Still, it saved us from a climb.

We finally arrived at the ferry port with just ten minutes to spare. That had been too close. The terminal was more a rickety old pier than an actual port. The ticket office was in a dilapidated old shed. We went in and bought our tickets. On display at the desk was a CD containing songs written and performed by the King himself. It seemed this King had many talents. One of them though, wasn't for marketing. He hadn't told anyone how much he wanted for the CDs.

We boarded the ferry and waited for them to load up with building supplies and boxes of ice cream for the shop. The ferry was small in comparison to the huge swells being conjured up by the strong winds. The Tory Sound is a notoriously rough stretch of ocean. As we headed out, the boat was thrown about like a piece of flotsam. To begin with, Anne and I stood at the front, but were soon driven back by the fierce winds and spray from the waves as they crashed against the sides of the boat. The deck was slowly turning into a river. The people around us each wore a look of sheer terror on their faces. All except one man, who was dressed in an Aran jumper, black jeans, wellington boots and had a black beanie pulled over his ears. He spent the entire journey with a huge, wide grin on his face. He turned out to be one of the island's workmen, and was therefore obviously used to this trip.

Tory Island is a remote place, situated eleven kilometres off the northern coast of Donegal. It is three miles long and half a mile wide. Its situation in the Tory Sound makes it extremely vulnerable to bad weather. All in all it is described as a bleak and inhospitable place. Nevertheless it has a population of 170 inhabitants living in two towns, imaginatively titled East Town and West Town. The island is famous for its school of painters. The most famous being the King himself. His and other people's paintings have been exhibited all over Europe and even in New York.

The pier at the other end was still being built. Once the boat was moored we disembarked and made our way along a muddy road until we reached a junction, which is actually the only one on the island. It also contained the only road signs on the island. These signs were in Gaelic so they weren't much help. Mind you with only two towns, each with the required direction in their names, signs were hardly needed.

What we did need was to find the *Radharc na Mara hostel*. I hadn't booked, figuring that a hostel on an island such as this was hardly likely to be full. I hadn't figured on the fact that the island would be full of construction workers. The hostel was indeed full. From there we were directed to various houses that were apparently B&Bs, although no signs were out front to indicate this. These were full of construction workers too. At each house we were directed to another. It was looking more and more like we were going to be marooned on this island: the ferry on which we had come over was the last of the day, and it had already left for its return journey. As I surveyed the area this idea became more and more unappealing. The landscape was extremely barren. The weather was cold, wet and windy. Also we were both cold and wet due to our ride on the front of the boat. As we stood there shivering and watching as the sky grew even darker with the setting of the sun, we both began to fear that we had made a dreadful mistake coming here. All this just to meet a King. He had better be worth it.

We had heard that the King often comes to meet visitors as they arrive on the island, as part of his royal duties. But today he was nowhere to be seen. A pity, I'd hoped he might have found room in his palace for two weary travellers. There was a hotel on the island, but I figured that would be far too expensive - forty pounds, I found out later.

Fortunately a little old lady called Mary came to our rescue.

Mary was a local woman who had two beds in a room upstairs. Two more rooms were attached to the back of this. One of those was taken by a French couple who had also come over on the boat. They had to come through our room to get to theirs; a fact they were very apologetic about. It didn't bother us. We thankfully changed out of our wet clothes and laid them about the room to dry. Later on we found them by the fire. Good old Mary, I thought. It was almost like staying with your grandma.

Tory Island has one pub, one café, one shop and a hotel bar. The café was perched on the top of a hill at the edge of town. We wandered in and took a seat by the window. Two young girls were sitting in the corner chatting in Gaelic. Once we had sat down, one of them came over and took our order.

The weather outside was growing steadily worse. Through the steamed up window we could see the bleak, wind-beaten landscape outside and hear the wind whistling and howling past the window. The clouds were becoming thicker and the rain looked set to get much worse. I watched in amazement as a small fishing boat was heading out to sea from the island, riding waves that must have been twice the height of the boat itself. I expressed my concern to the girl who had taken our order. 'Oh it's all right, often the smaller boats can navigate the waves better,' she said.

In winter no one can get to and from the island for weeks at a time. I was told that back in the 80s a storm that lasted for months rendered the two towns devoid of electricity, and cut off all communications to the island. After this many of the inhabitants apparently applied for relocation to the main-land. The government had been trying to move all the islanders off for a long time, and this storm had helped some. But still the more stubborn ones remained and refused to budge.

The island is predominantly Gaelic speaking. The two young girls running the café were happily switching between the two. They explained to us that they go to school on the mainland during the winter, but have to spend their summers here. They didn't like it and couldn't wait until they were old enough to leave. I couldn't blame them really. After all, there was literally nothing to do.

At least tonight we had a valid excuse for going to the pub. There was nothing else to do. And it was cold outside. The wind howled across the barren landscape and the town's muddy roads were devoid of life when we left the café and made our way to *Club Soisialta (Social Club)*, the local pub. As the evening progressed the pub slowly filled up. Along with the French couple from the B&B, an old man also joined us for a while. Huey was one of the islanders, but had moved away many years ago. He was back here now to look after his sick mother. She was very old and probably didn't have much longer to live. When she is gone, he plans to return to the mainland. He said that the island is just too isolated for someone like him. I imagined that could well be a problem for a lot of people here. It must take a special kind of person to actually want to live here.

As the evening progressed our hopes that the King would come into the pub that night and play some music seemed more and more likely to be dashed. The locals said that he usually comes in late. But by the end of the evening he still hadn't turned up; well the end of our evening anyway. Despite this we'd had a good night. The pub had filled up

w'.h the many locals and all the workmen, and they all
d. nced and drank the night away to jukebox music.

After stumbling through the pitch-black, muddy streets at
god-knows what time in the morning, we made it back to the
B&B. One of the workmen who had walked with us was also
staying at Mary's place. The fire was still roaring in the front
room as we entered, so we sat down by it and chatted with
our new friend. He was from County Tyrone in Northern
Ireland, and seemed to know a lot about Tory. He told us that
the islanders are paid double dole or pension to live here. He
also said that people like Mary make more on top with the
B&B business. They have plenty of money but nothing to
spend it on. Most of them just sleep, drink and paint. He said
you can buy a house for around £2500, but only if you had
been born on the island or have relatives living here. The
locals are not tempted by money. Our workman/tourist guide
had tried to buy one, in the hope of selling it at a huge profit. He'd even offered a higher price than was being asked, but
no one would sell to him. They weren't interested in the
money; they just wanted to preserve the culture of the
islanders. How nice it is to know that there are still some
things that money can't buy. Eventually our newfound friend
shooed us off to bed, saying that he wanted to sit by the fire
alone and think.

Fine!

The next morning we took a stroll to East Town. The
weather hadn't changed a bit; still cold, windy and overcast.
But at least it wasn't raining. The north-eastern side of the
island is dominated by high cliffs that were being constantly
pounded by the huge waves below. A lone caravan sat rotting
amid the cold and barren landscape stretching out before us.
It seemed to perfectly illustrate the loneliness of this island.

However, there was something quite alluring about it all. The bleakness and cold afforded a sort of unusual beauty. I read in the guidebook that the cliffs were home to many puffins. But when we got to East Town it started to rain. I had stupidly forgotten my raincoat. This was just the kind of place where you should always have it with you. I got soaked. East Town was nothing more than a residential area. I had wanted to continue on to find these puffins, but the rain drove us back to the B&B for yet another change of clothes.

After warming ourselves by the fire in the hotel bar for a while, we set out to see the island's art exhibition. Many of the locals' paintings are on display in the community hall. It was closed when we arrived, but a passing local went and got the owner who then came and opened up for us to look around. Now I'm no expert on art, but these paintings were good. The bleak atmosphere of the island was captured beautifully in many of these paintings. I usually have a very low boredom threshold when looking at such things, but here I found myself fascinated.

We then set out to meet the King. The French couple joined us too. The obvious place to look was his palace; his palace being a nice little house on the hill near to the café. As we approached his front door I wondered what I should say. After all, it's not as though I've ever knocked for a King before. As we all stood there on the doorstep eagerly waiting to be ushered in, a smiling old lady answered the door.

'Hello,' I said. 'Is the King there?'

Now I think I can say with all sincerity, that is probably the only time I will ever utter such a sentence for as long as I live.

'No he's not, I'm sorry,' she replied. 'He went down to the art gallery. If you wander down there I'm sure you will bump into him.'

On an island this size it would be difficult not to, yet so far it hadn't happened.

Down at the pier we spotted an old man dressed in wellington boots, a blue raincoat and wearing a black cap. He fitted the description well, so we wandered over. When he spotted us he waved and came to meet us.

'Are you the King of Tory?' asked Anne.

'That I am!' he replied.

After hearty handshakes and introductions he explained that he had seen Anne yesterday but was busy working on some paintings for an upcoming exhibition. It seemed he had come into the pub shortly after we had left. Just our luck. I should have guessed that the pub would stay open most of the night.

He left us for a moment as he went to see off the first wave of tourists about to leave on the boat, which weren't many it seemed. The French couple went on this boat, so we said goodbye to them and waited. When he had finished, he returned and spent about half an hour chatting with us and posing for photos. Patsy was quite a character: chatty, friendly, helpful and with a fantastic sense of humour. He gave us a brief rundown on the island and its inhabitants, and explained that English was his second language and he wasn't as confident with it as he was with Gaelic. He sounded all right to me. He enjoyed his role as King and said that he always tries his best to meet everyone who visits the island. He took his royal duties seriously - as seriously as could be expected, I suppose. Most evenings he would entertain visitors in the pub with his music. We had been unfortunate enough to be there on a night when he was too busy. After a lengthy chat he bade us farewell and promised to see us off on our boat.

Anne and I went to the pub and had one for the sea. Then we collected our stuff, said goodbye to Mary and her husband and wandered down to the pier. True to his word, the King came down and saw us off with a hearty farewell. As the King and his island shrank off into the distance I realised that this was one place I would be returning to. The remoteness, the bleak weather and the barren, inhospitable look about it, had a strange attraction. I could understand why it was a haven for painters. It had a sort of cold beauty. And it was the perfect getaway. Also it contained great people. One of the girls from the café had gone out of her way to get Anne some sea sickness pills for the journey home, which she had taken with her Guinness. She was now clinging on to the rails in a sort of trance-like state.

Well, we had achieved our objective of meeting the King of Tory. Was it worth the long, and quite perilous, journey? I think it was. How often do you get to meet a King? And how often do you get to see an island like that? But even though he wasn't officially a King, he was a kind and helpful man. The way he welcomes you to his island and the hospitality he extends, makes him, in reality, a true King of Hearts.

__14__

Mad Dogs and an Englishman

Instead of going back to Magheroarty, we were taking the ferry to Bunbeg. After a perilous journey across the Tory Sound we rounded the north-western corner of the mainland and suddenly found the huge waves had subsided. The reason for this was that a series of islands along this section of coast shelter it from the rough sea. Also the clouds had cleared. The blazing evening sun lit up the surrounding sea and enhanced the immense beauty of this coastline. We were surrounded by unspoilt golden beaches and low green hills. The coastline was scattered with tiny whitewashed villages. If it hadn't been for the cold, this could quite easily have passed for a little Caribbean harbour.

Bunbeg harbour was so small and packed that we had to moor next to a barge and climb across to disembark. Our skipper told us there was a hostel around the corner. 'Knock on the first house,' he said.

We did just that, and no one answered. Next door to the house was a huge building called *Tir na Nog*. A sign on the front advertised self-catering apartments. No one answered there either. The harbour stretched around the corner and formed the centre of the area we were in. Across this harbour was Bunbeg House. Andy, the proprietor, was also a famous character from the Fridge Book. Three people, who were having dinner on their yacht, told us to go see him and he would phone the hostel owner. It seemed we were becoming fridge groupies.

Bunbeg House was a beautiful B&B with a restaurant and bar attached, sitting right on the waterfront. Andy himself came to the bar as we entered. We explained our predicament and he phoned the owner.

'You must be Andy,' I said, when he returned from making the phone call.

It seemed he was used to this star treatment. Andy was a major feature in the book after offering the author free accommodation, and also helping him immensely when he was trying to get to Tory Island. At the time the ferry was not operating.

Andy was always pleased to meet his fans, as he called us. He lent over to us and covered the side of his mouth. '"There's more of my fans here," I tell my girls,' he whispered, as he nodded his head towards the kitchen where his two teenage assistants were working. He then insisted that we come back for a drink later. How could we refuse?

Tir na Nog was actually the hostel that our skipper had been talking about. The owner was in fact Andy's father in law. He reminded me of an old bloke I'd once worked for in Australia. Both were men with pots of money who seemed to prefer to spend it on beer, cigarettes and food, rather than on decent clothes for themselves. Greg, the Australian, was a compulsive chain smoker. I don't think I can ever recall one instance when he didn't have a cigarette hanging from his mouth or burning into his lip. He also had the ability to have an entire conversation with you and never once remove the cigarette from his mouth in the process. The only time his hand made contact was to light the end or stub out the butt in the ashtray. Then he would light another. You always knew how to find him. Simply follow the trail of ash and you would eventually come across him. I was doing an impression of him one evening when my cousin dared me to smoke the whole cigarette like he does. In other words not take it out of my mouth. I did it, but was severely ill afterwards. The smoke filled my lungs, drifted up my nose and smothered my eyes. To this day I can never understand just how he could smoke like that.

He showed us to our room, which was a private room with two beds. It seemed that this wasn't really a hostel but, as the sign explained, self-catering apartments. He charged us only £10.00 each, so it was well worth it. The room was basic, just the beds and an en-suite toilet, and a lovely view of the harbour from the window. Downstairs was a large kitchen and television room. All in all, it wasn't half bad.

We were the only guests in the Tir na Nog. The main reason for this was that the old boy didn't advertise. In fact he didn't really do much. It was more of a hobby for him nowadays. He said it was up for sale, but only to the right customer. He hated the fact that big hotels rip people off with their extortionate prices. He didn't want his place turned into that. Also he didn't want the area to be overtaken by tourism. At the moment it was a small, quiet harbour and he wanted it to stay that way. I could understand that; the area was more beautiful than I had anticipated. Therefore he was in no rush to sell the place. It's not very often you meet a rich man with morals. The downside was that he wasn't really bothering with the upkeep of the place. In fact the only things he took care of in the whole building were the plants. He came in daily and pottered around watering and clipping them. They got better treatment than the guests, it seemed.

We settled in and then took a walk into town, which soon turned out to be a damn sight longer than we had thought it would be. This part of the world really was rural Ireland. County Donegal stretches further north than anywhere else in Northern Ireland, and one third of the region is Irish speaking – these areas are known as Gaeltacht regions. As in the Aran Islands and Tory Island, in these areas Irish is more widely spoken than English. Tourism here is very seasonal. Apparently outside of summer the entire county is virtually shut down and asleep. Weather wise it's not a great place to be in winter.

However now was not winter, and the weather was gorgeous. It was a lovely evening as we strolled along the country road which ended at the junction for Bunbeg High Street. Bunbeg High Street was no more than a pub, a small shop and a sparse scattering of other small businesses. It was hardly the busiest of high streets. Bunbeg, Derrybeg and Gweedore virtually run into each other. The villages were once again more like areas with the buildings scattered across a vast area, with plenty of space to spare. The only real activity was the occasional youth speeding back and forth along the road in his turbo-charged car, trying to impress the local girls. I could well imagine that there wasn't a lot else to do. We found a little takeaway and had a bite to eat before popping in the nearby pub for a pint so Anne could obtain the bus times for the next day. We then returned to Andy's little bar for a drink, where he quite happily signed my copy of the

Fridge Book.

The weather the next day was gorgeous. Andy explained that this part of Ireland is so sheltered that the summer is often like this.

'We had a huge storm here in Donegal a few years back, and it completely missed us here. We didn't know anything about it until the locals mentioned it,' said Andy.

Anne decided to head off today and make her way back to Galway. She was running short of money and couldn't afford to hang around. Andy was in the process of setting up a sailing club and offered her a job for the summer, as she was a qualified sailor. However, the more she thought about it the more she decided that she would soon get bored around here. Regardless of how beautiful it is, there really isn't a lot to do; as we had seen the evening before.

The gorgeous weather, coupled with the tranquillity of this beautiful harbour, was the only invitation I needed to kick back for a few days. The harbour was about a mile off the main road where Anne had to catch the bus. Foolishly being a gentleman, I offered to accompany Anne there and pull her bag for her. I fought a constant battle between keeping the bag upright and fighting off the flies. The flies were prolific, and there seemed no stopping them. Why they all chose me and not Anne, I'll never know. (No funny comments please!).

After seeing Anne off, I returned to the harbour, sat myself down on the edge and took some photographs and wrote in my journal. Andy was across the other side attempting to get his new Zodiac launched. At low tide, the water drops a good two metres. It is impossible to launch anything. It was just starting to come in now and Andy was determined to get out. When he was ready he invited me along. I didn't need asking twice. Along with his three children, we were joined by Mike and Gayle, who were staying at his B&B. As we rode out of the harbour he told me to sit at the front, assuring me it was safe, because he wanted to distribute the weight about the boat.

Boy that thing was fast! Once clear of the harbour, Andy opened up the throttle. That little boat shot into the bay like a bullet from a gun. As my legs levitated from the floor, the only thing keeping me from being flung over the side was a couple of rubber hand-holds, and a tenacious grip on my part. Andy, it seemed, was quite the boy racer in his boat. I guess like the youths in their cars, this is the only real excitement he gets here. For the next fifteen minutes Andy swirled, spun and flipped his little Zodiac in all manner of directions; making it look like a seal high on drugs. Eventually though, he seemed to remember that he had guests on his boat – not to mention his own children – and managed to get a hold of himself.

Andy then took us on a leisurely tour of the many surrounding islands. No one inhabited these islands anymore. Like Tory Island they were once populated, but the government had persuaded these people to move ashore. On each island were the remains of tiny villages; ghost towns now. But nevertheless they are still pretty much intact. Andy pulled up on one of these islands so we could have a look around. We moored at the disused pier. Now it seemed it was used for business purposes. One of Ireland's dishes, believe it or not, is seaweed. A young couple were collecting the seaweed and had laid it out on the pier to dry. It was broken into small pieces and spread out across a large area, regularly being turned by these two. When ready it would be packaged and sent to supermarkets across the country.

I spent that evening in Andy's bar. For the most part he'd sit on our side of the bar and socialise with his customers. Every now and then he popped back to serve someone. His B&B was pretty full. He had a group of Germans staying who wanted to hear traditional Irish music, and so he was doing his best to find them some cassettes. The bar was quite small and cosy and afforded a lovely view of the harbour. I quite liked it, and was to spend much of my time here.

Andy loved working here. He was from London originally and had married an Irish woman and moved here to set up this business. The first years had been extremely difficult. Business dries up totally in the winter. In fact he closes the B&B altogether. He explained that during the winter he would run up a debt of thousands, which he would pay off during the summer months. The same would happen again the next year. As the years went by the debt became less and less. Now he was in a position to reap the rewards of his hard work, hence the Zodiac. He had also invested in a few small yachts in order to start up his small sailing club. The future was looking very bright. His involvement in the Fridge Book hadn't done him any harm either. He had two copies proudly on display behind his bar. I took the opportunity to add a stain to the rapidly growing collection in the back of my copy.

Later on that evening we were joined by Kevin from Belfast. He had left his wife and child to sleep and come down for a night-cap. We drank and discussed, among other things, the possible reasons for stout being better here than in England. Andy's suggestion was that the cellar is closer to the taps here in Ireland. Thus there is less piping between the barrel and the tap, and so less beer is left sitting in the pipes between servings. Also the coolers were directly underneath the taps. At two o'clock in the morning we all staggered off to bed to sleep off our theories.

Yet again it was a gorgeous day. I took the long walk to Bunbeg High Street. From there I walked down to the beach. As Andy had pointed out the day before, the harbours and inlets are extremely shallow in places. It was low tide and the beach area was a field of sand the size of a baseball pitch. In the middle lay a wrecked boat. It wasn't very big and I think it was just left there to lend character to the area. As I stood in the middle of this giant sand pit I scanned the surrounding scenery: islands with golden sandy beaches, green hills with a small scattering of houses, a mountain shimmering in the distant mist, wind turbines on the distant hills, and a massive ugly tourist hotel across the road. Why? It looked so out of place here in this vast stretch of natural beauty. Sometimes I despair at the mentality of the human race. In a sense, I can understand the reason for having this. But why build something so plain and ugly? Why not design something that at least fits in to the landscape and helps add character? Not make eyesores. The mind boggles. I shrugged this all off and passed the rest of the day wandering around the area, taking in the wonderful views and wandering the lonely hills. Once again, in the evening I drank in Andy's bar.

The next morning I decided to head to Westport. I had to catch the 7.30 bus to Sligo and change there. Feda O'Donnell is the main bus company serving this area. As I trotted along the road, fighting the flies, I was joined by a dog. I don't know where he came from but he followed me all the way to the main road and stayed with me until the bus came. I was actually glad of the company. It seems even the dogs here are devoid of excitement. As we waited for the bus, my four-legged friend seemed to find it fun to play chicken with all the passing cars. He would sit there quite happily, until his sensitive ears pricked up to the sound of an oncoming car. He would then position himself by the side of the road, facing towards the oncoming vehicle. As it rounded the corner he would jump out in front. Most swerved or stopped, but a few of them, probably locals who are used to it, drove on. He would then jump back to the side and make a gallant display of chasing it up the road. I'm not sure who I feared for most.

At Sligo I had four hours to kill before catching the next bus. I spent the time wandering around. It was quite a pleasant little place. The town's claim to fame is of Ireland's most celebrated poet, William Butler Yeats. Although he was born in Dublin, his mother was from Sligo and he spent much of his childhood here. Many of his poems are linked to this part of Ireland. There is a sculpture outside the Ulster Bank that contains his poetry inscribed all over his body. It seemed like a nice little town, but I didn't feel that there was all that much to keep me here.

Four hours later I was sitting at the back of the bus when I was surprised to see Anne get on and take a seat at the front. I wandered down and returned the surprise. She then came back and joined me. It appeared that she had got the offer of a tour around Sligo on the back of a motorbike, and had decided to stay another day. She was going to Westport as well, so it looked like we were to be travel partners once again.

Upon arrival in Westport we tried the Old Mill Hostel, but it was full. The other was quite far out of town, so Anne phoned them on her mobile – handy travelling with a posh backpacker at times. They had two beds left and said they would hold them for ten minutes. Their generosity was just too much.

The hostel turned out to be very big and extremely impersonal. The German at reception did his utmost to let you know that he couldn't give a shit about you or where you were from. Anne got a room with three rude German women, while I got a small dorm with eight beds crammed inside. It was a complete nightmare. I had to climb over people's baggage to get to the free bed in the corner. There was no room on the floor so I had to dump my bag on the armchair crammed between two of the bunks. On the upside though, the people in the dorm were very friendly.

Anne and I hit the pubs that night. First of all we went to Matt Molloy's pub. Sitting in the corner we were befriended by Peter. Peter was originally from Dublin but now lived in Westport. He preferred it here. 'Dublin's like a big village,' he said, 'Everybody knows your business.'

He had been drinking since two that afternoon and ended the evening early with a cup of coffee. Peter managed one of the many pubs in town and offered us both work there. We thanked him, but declined.

When Peter left we wandered down to another pub. The only two seats available were at a table full of people. We sat there. Before we had even spoken to them, we were offered a cigarette. It was the perfect ice breaker and soon we were ushered in on their conversation. They were all part of the same family. The mother and father were originally from Dublin but had moved here.

'It's much nicer here than Dublin,' said the father. 'Here they are much friendlier and more considerate. If a man drinks too much and falls asleep at the bar, the barman will let him sleep it off. "Ah he's grand," he'll just say. "He works hard, let him sleep it off" When he wakes up the barman will get him a strong cup of coffee and arrange him a ride home. Now in Dublin they would drag him out and he would be the talk of the town for weeks.'

The grandmother of the family still lived in Dublin and was here for the weekend. She agreed that it was nicer here. We told them what we were doing in Ireland and mentioned that we kept meeting up by accident.

'Ah! It's destiny, so it is!' said the father.

A few years ago I might have agreed with him. But after my experiences of travelling, this was becoming a common occurrence.

The two teenage girls at the table were getting restless and decided to find a night-club.

'They're going to get shifted,' said the grandmother.

'What!' I exclaimed, shocked by her frankness when it came to her young granddaughters.

They all laughed and explained that the word 'shifted' in Ireland, means to get a kiss.

Now that's a new one.

___15___

A Pub Crawl of Letterfrack

I decided to try my luck at hitch hiking again. The section of land between here and Galway is called the Connemara. I wanted to get to a small village called Letterfrack. Anne was taking a bus to Galway. She had an interview with a costume company on Monday morning. So we said goodbye, again, and I headed off to find a suitable spot for hitching.

The road out of Westport was quite narrow and there weren't many suitable spots. My only option was at the edge of a T-junction. I figured it might prove a difficult place for people to stop, if they wanted to. It was Sunday and very quiet. I had the feeling I'd be here for a very a long time. However, five minutes and two cars later I was picked up by Kevin and Sabrina from Switzerland. They screeched to a halt and reversed back for me.

The car was small, but they went to great effort to fit me in. The boot was full, so Kevin put my backpack on the back shelf. I pointed out that the pack would obscure his view out the back window.

'It's okay,' he said, 'I use this mirror,' pointing to the rear view mirror in the front.

I felt it prudent not to question as to how this would make any difference.

The two of them were on a two-week holiday. It transpired that they had seen me walking through the town with my backpack on and had wondered if I was Swiss, as earlier in their trip they had met a backpacker who had been from Switzerland. On that conjecture they'd decided to pick me up. A curious way of thinking, but fortunate for me. Thankfully when they found out I was in fact English and not Swiss, they didn't throw me out the car.

The road to Letterfrack took us through thirty-five kilometres of fantastic scenery. It wound its way through pale green mountain valleys and along large lakes enshrouded in mist. Just before arriving in Letterfrack we passed the stunningly beautiful Kylemore Abbey, set aside a beautiful lake and entrenched at the base of a lush green hill.

Letterfrack was nothing more than a crossroads. It consisted of one shop, a restaurant, a few B&Bs and three pubs. Each pub was situated on a corner of the crossroads. There didn't appear to be any residential areas. It was raining when I was dropped off, so I threw on my raincoat and headed up a gravel road to the *Old Monastery Hostel*. Once inside I was shown to my dorm and waited out the rain in the common room. The hostel dog lay sprawled out across the sofa and sitting at the table was an Australian girl, Abby, and a Chinese-looking guy, Tim, who was in fact from Holland. Abby was thinking about working here in Letterfrack. She told me that she really liked it here.

'But there's nothing here by the look of it,' I said.

'That's why I like it,' she replied.

Fair enough.

When the rain stopped I made my way outside. The entrance to the Connemara National Park was just outside the village. I wandered down to it and then up a hill to a queue of cars waiting to pay. I joined them – not wanting to push ahead – and idly wondered what they would all think when they saw a guy shuffling along on foot behind them.

At the kiosk I smiled my best smile and asked if I could get a discount for being on foot. It wasn't to be though, so I delved into my pocket and pulled out a pitiful handful of change. She must have felt sorry for me and let me in for a pound.

The visitor centre has three-dimensional models and large scale displays of the Connemara and its landscape, giving all information on the area's flora, fauna and geology. The national park is a 2000-hectare piece of land containing bogs, mountains and heath. I was handed a leaflet by a very nice lady and told of the various walks around the area. I decided to take one of the walks.

At the entrance to the first trail was a sign that read:

**Please keep on the marked trail,
and please do not interfere with the ponies.**

I wondered if the latter was a problem around here. Looking at the size of Letterfrack Village, this could well have been the case. The lack of women, and the ensuing loneliness, might well have caused them to look elsewhere.

('Come ere mi lovely! Now you're a fine looking mare, aren't yer?')

I ignored the warning to stay on the trail and paid the price with wet feet and the fear of being lost in a swamp forever. I didn't fancy being dug up in years to come and put on show as a warning to adhere to that sign.

The park experiences a mild climate due to its proximity to the Atlantic Ocean. Storms that brew up in the Atlantic and are blown this way, end up being released over this part of Ireland because it's the first major landmass it reaches. Therefore rainfall is plentiful with an average precipitation of 1600 mm falling on 250 rain days. The result is a well irrigated landscape.

Perhaps a bit too well.

I had climbed a large hill and ended up in a similar situation to the one back in Baltimore – you would think I'd have the sense to learn from my mistakes, wouldn't you? Each step I made was like treading on a wet sponge. I made my way slowly and carefully down the hill and back to the main path, and continued on this way.

Later I discovered the staff entrance to the park was just outside the hostel. After all that I could have sneaked in for free.

It was still fairly early in the day, so I decided to take a walk along the road and see what was outside the village. Again I adopted a dog who accompanied me all the way. It was a big black Labrador. The dogs in this part of Ireland seem to all like playing chicken with the passing cars. Once again I was in fear of the dog or the passengers getting hurt. I tried my best to entice him away, but to no avail. He followed me right the way out of the village and on to the next one. This village was set beside a lake. The Connemara hills formed the backdrop to this lake, and also the reflection. It was without doubt an area of immense beauty. It was also a good spot to keep my newfound friend away from passing cars.

On the way back he resumed his confrontations with the passing traffic. As we approached the entrance to the National Park, a woman started to pull out. The dog leapt in front and assumed his attack posture. The woman braked hard and the dog, knowing he had the upper hand, remained in front barking and growling.

'Would you control your dog!' she shouted at me.

'It's not my dog,' I said with a shrug, and left him to it.

Later that evening I befriended a couple of German girls in the hostel. They explained that they were on holiday and had both become ill with Bronchitis. How's that for bad luck? Because of this they politely refused my offer of a drink down the pub.

Sitting in the corner was an American reading a book and murmuring to himself every now and then. When I went to the dorm to get my boots, he was sprawled out on the floor in a semi-splits position. I invited him to the pub and his refusal was the best I'd heard yet.

'I've drunk so much beer on this trip that my body is starting to reject it. I think that after a while your body develops an immunity to the alcohol.'

In other words he couldn't handle his beer.

With no one else in the hostel, I decided to go alone. I figured I'd embark on a pub crawl of Letterfrack – not too difficult given the number of pubs. The first was a hangout for the older generation – the bloke next to me sporting an incredibly dodgy wig was testimony to that. The next pub was empty, aside from one couple talking to the barmaid. With two beers inside me and having experienced a total lack of excitement I was all set to return to the hostel and go to sleep, or start jumping out in the road and chasing passing cars. But I had set out to sample all of the pubs – and after all there was only one more to go. So I figured I ought to at least complete my pub crawl.

The last pub was the one attached to the restaurant. I stepped through the door and was met by the sight of a large crowd of people drinking and laughing. It seemed that this was where all the action was. Abby and Tim were also there. They introduced me to a Kiwi couple, also staying at the hostel. The reason I hadn't seen them earlier was because they slept all day and drank all night. I ended up leaving that bar at one in the morning.

The hostel offered a free breakfast, and it was downstairs in the basement. It consisted of a pot of slop – sorry, porridge – organic scones and a strange squashy type of bread which looked far too healthy for my liking. All this was taken to Blues music. Now I love Blues with a passion, but it's hardly the sort of music to get you motivated in the morning, now is it? So I had another cup of coffee.

I wanted to get to Clifden, which was twelve kilometres down the road. I decided to hitch again. Ten minutes after assuming the position an estate van with German plates came out of the hostel junction and pulled over. Tim was sitting in the front. A thickset man wearing glasses jumped out and shot me a look of annoyance.

'You should have asked me earlier,' he snorted.

'I didn't know you were going!' I replied.

I didn't even know who he was.

He flung the boot open and motioned for me to put my pack inside. I did, and then jumped in the back seat to find Abby sitting next to me, looking strangely serene.

'How are you feeling this morning?' I asked.

'Fine!' she replied, her eyes displaying the effects of the

substance that was quite obviously making her feel that way.

Abby and Tim quite happily chatted to me, Tim giving a warning to avoid a certain hostel. The driver never said a word to me, he just drove like a maniac. When he dropped us all off I thanked him, but he just ignored me. So even though he had been kind enough to give me a lift to Clifden, I still had no choice but to declare him an ignorant shit.

Clifden is capital of the Connemara region. The *Clifden Town Hostel* was just across the road, and looked extremely inviting. The owner bore a striking resemblance to the actor Michael Keaton. He was extremely helpful and told me about all the various walks or cycling trips I could do.

The weather had taken a turn for the better today, and due to the heat I just took a short walk. Clifden is set aside two lovely inlets. The blue sky was reflected in the shallow bays and lit up the low green hill forming the backdrop to the village. The walk followed the bay area and took me along low cliffs and into large fields towards the ruins of an old castle. I took my time, after all there was nothing to rush for.

On the way back I spotted one of those Pekinese dogs – you know, the ones who look like they've been running repeatedly into the patio doors when closed. It, too, was playing chicken with the passing traffic. It seemed that in the dog kingdom of Ireland, size doesn't matter when it comes to attacking motor vehicles. A show of aggression is all that's needed. I wondered if the parents passed on their techniques to the pups, making it a family tradition, or whether they went to a special school to learn these techniques.

"Now pay attention lads, there's a lot to be learnt before you can go out by yourselves."

__16__

New Shoes

I took a bus to Galway and returned to Kinlay House. I only intended to stay for a day and then take a bus to Dublin. Once I had got the information I needed, I spent the day wandering around taking pictures.

The hostel was situated on the corner of Eyre Square, in the middle of which stood a large park. Opposite the park was the Eyre Square Centre. Throughout this shopping centre I found a display from the World Press Photography. Boards were dotted periodically throughout the centre. I wandered idly through, captivated totally by what I saw. Some of the pictures were incredible. The one that most caught my eye was of a businessman in Johannesburg about to shoot a thief who had stolen his mobile phone. He had him cornered in a back alley and the thief was lying on the floor, a look of terror showing plainly on his face. The businessman had the gun aimed at him, his face displaying a look of insane rage. You could tell his finger was just seconds away from yanking that trigger. Split second timing. However, it appeared that the click of the camera distracted the business-man momentarily and he turned the gun on the cameraman. By this time the police had arrived and apprehended them both. The cameraman's actions had undoubtedly saved the thief's life.

Another amazing set of pictures showed a Muslim sect chasing a man through the streets. The man was believed to have been part of a group who had attacked their Mosque. Each picture showed him being pelted to death with bricks and stones. The last was undoubtedly the most disturbing. The man lay on the ground, bruised, cut, mutilated, and very dead. Despite this man being dead, one of the attackers was leaning over the body, poised with a knife on his throat and ready to slit it open. The first thought that springs to mind is, how the hell can someone photograph that and not do some-thing? But then again, what can you do? You could never fight an angry mob like that on your own, and would more than likely end up dead yourself. Maybe by capturing it on film and bringing it to the attention of the world, the photographer is doing more to help? It's something to think about.

I finally managed to tear myself away from the photographs and went for a walk through the town. Wandering through the streets, I bumped into Anne once again. We were no longer surprised by this. We went for a coffee and brought each other up to date. She was going to do a day's work at the place where she'd had the interview, and see how it went. We met again later that evening for a drink.

Anne chose a nice pub in the centre of town. The major-ity of the pub had been sectioned off into what were known as little snugs. These were single tables walled in so small groups, or lovers, could drink and talk in private. Anne and I sat at the bar. On the edge of the bar top there was guttering.

When someone asked what it was for, I suggested that it was there to catch the spilt beer and direct it into the barrel for the Budweiser tap.

'No,' chuckled the barmaid. 'It's for customers to rest their arms in.' She nodded towards me as she said this.

Taking the hint I removed my arms from the guttering.

After many pints I said goodbye to Anne, yet again, and returned to my hostel. That night my sleep was rudely interrupted again by the fire alarm. In the morning I caught a Citylink bus to Dublin for five pounds. I know that longer journeys are often better value, but here it seemed even cheaper. I could travel the width of the country for less than it costs to travel to the next county.

A Canadian girl back in Galway had recommended the Ashfield House Hostel. In my years of travelling I have learned that recommendations from other travellers were the best advice you could take. These people had been there recently, and would most certainly tell you if it was bad. In fact they would delight in doing so.

For the first time I made my way through the centre of Ireland. From what I could see it was mostly farmland, green fields and small villages. Ireland was certainly living up to its nickname, the Emerald Isle. Every bus trip I had taken so far had taken me through stunning vistas of rich, vividly green fields, often stretching as far as the eye could see. I never seemed to tire of looking at this wonderful landscape. And when the sun came out, which I confess wasn't that often, these fields seemed to glow. Each village we passed through reflected this bright landscape. The buildings had been painted in various pastel colours. On the way we passed through the town of Kilcock. A sign on a lamppost read:

Kilcock,
toxic waste,
what do you think?

It didn't look that bad to me.

After five weeks in rural Ireland, Dublin came as quite a shock: people everywhere, pushing past and getting in my way. Instantly I hated it. I yearned for the relaxed pace of life I had been used to: the casual atmosphere, the friendliness, people saying hello to you in the street or waving at you from their car. I realised there and then that I would only be staying one day; my dorm bed costing £12.50 confirmed this. However the recommendation had been a good one, and Ashfield House really was a nice place to stay. It was convenient too. The bus had dropped me off in O'Connell Street, by the River Liffey. The hostel wasn't in my guidebook but the Canadian girl had circled the street for me. A quick look at the map proved that all I had to do was cross the bridge and walk a few metres and I was there. The location couldn't have been more convenient.

The one good thing about cities is that it's a good place to shop. Invariably you can also find good bargains. The immense gaping holes in the soles of my boots were a sign that maybe this was a good time to get some new ones. I found a pair in a sale, extremely cheap. Now what I did next proved to be the fatal mistake: I threw my old ones away. In a grand ceremony on the streets of Dublin I tossed them in a nearby bin then went for a walk, proudly sporting my new shiny boots. I figured that as I only had one day, I should see as much as I could. I walked for hours, along the Liffey, through the shopping precinct of Grafton Street, Temple Bar and to Dublin Castle. It was a long day, broken only by a short break to pop into a nearby pub for a pint of Guinness. There was no atmosphere in the pub, and the price was much higher. Mind you it was the afternoon. Dublin is nicknamed Fair City. I had to admit, as cities go, it was quite attractive. I did enjoy wandering its streets.

By the end of the day my feet were screaming with agony. Back at the hostel I removed my new boots to reveal a set of large multiple blisters. I thought it quite ironic that after all the walking I had done in my old boots, especially on the Beara Peninsula, that a little bit of walking around a city in new ones could have rendered me the image of an old man who'd had a slight accident in his underpants.

The dorm was quite cramped. Sleeping with a Dutchman's smelly feet in my face, wasn't the most pleasant experience of my life. I rose bright and early and annoyed them all with my packing. It couldn't be helped. I did try to do it quietly, but that only seemed to make things worse. Once packed I took full benefit of the hostel's free breakfast and then hobbled off to the bus station. I took a bus to Kilkenny and hobbled off to find the hostel.

__17__

<u>Gypsies, Handicaps and Bad Feet</u>

It was such a relief to get out of the city. The Ormande Hostel turned out to be just a short walk from the main bus station, although somehow I managed to miss it and walk the entire length of the road before realising that I had missed it and thus had to walk all the way back again. At reception I was greeted by a friendly old man who proceeded to check me in and show me to my room. Inside I got talking to my only roommate, Randy from Montreal. He was a bit bewildered because a group of English girls staying here had been laughing at his name. The girls, as it transpired, were part of a Welsh choir over here for a performance.

Kilkenny Town is fairly small. Situated either side of the River Nore, it's an attractive place with around 20,000 inhabitants. As I wandered down towards the river I spotted a sign advertising the Kilkenny Shopping Mall. It was a row of just four shops. Obviously a very optimistic outlook from one of the town planners.

From the bridge across the river I discovered the magnificent view of one of the three surviving towers of Kilkenny Castle, just a few yards away. The castle was originally begun in 1172 by Richard de Clare, who, according to the guidebook, was the Anglo-Norman conqueror of Ireland and better known as Strongbow. Mr Strongbow built a single wooden tower on the site. It wasn't until twenty years later that his son-in-law erected the castle with four towers in its place. In 1391 the castle was bought by the immensely wealthy and powerful Butler family. Their descendants continued to live there until 1935. However, even with their immense wealth, maintaining such a place became too much of a financial strain for the Butler family. I dread to think what the heating bill was alone. The furnishing was sold at auction and – this is the best part – the castle itself was sold to the city in 1967 for the whopping sum of £50. The Butler family really must have been in dire straits.

The castle is being restored to its original splendour. For a small fee you can enter the castle and take a forty-minute tour. Attached to the rear of the castle is twenty hectares of parkland with a Celtic cross-shaped rose garden centred around a large fountain. Entry to the grounds were free, so I spent my time there and admired the outside of the building. Considering that the city council only paid £50 for this castle, you'd have thought they would have allowed you entrance for free. Honestly, some people are just so greedy.

Just like any other town in Ireland, one thing Kilkenny wasn't short of was pubs. I sampled a couple of them that evening. Kilkenny's most obvious claim to fame is the beer of the same name. In the first pub I ordered a pint and was shocked to find that it cost way more than the average pint in Ireland. I had been paying around £2.20 for a pint of stout, or even ale. My pint of Kilkenny cost me £2.75. It was well worth it, though. I'd first tasted this beer in Australia a few years before, and had yearned to try it again since.

As I sipped my pint a woman walked in off the street and sat next to me. She was frail-looking with wild hair and a pointed face. She looked at me. 'Hello,' she said, with a glazed look in her eyes. 'Are ye alright?'

I nodded. 'I'm fine,' I replied.

She turned to the barmaid and said something incoherently to her. I wasn't sure if she was already incredibly drunk, or mentally incapacitated when it came to speech. The barmaid quite obviously didn't have a clue what she'd said. It took another barmaid and much repetition of the question to deduce that she wanted a Paddy's whiskey. When her drink arrived she slumped herself at the bar, sipped it, then turned and said to me, again: 'Hello. Are ye alright?'

I nodded once more, sped up my drinking and made a hasty exit to another pub. I spent the rest of the evening alone, but at least I had music to listen to.

My feet were still incredibly sore, so I stayed another day with the intention of resting them. The weather was gorgeous. This part of Ireland is known as the Sunny Southeast. Well, so far it was certainly living up to its name. I spent most of the day by the river, shoes and socks off and trousers rolled up.

On the way back, I popped into the pub for a pint of Kilkenny and something to eat. The barmaid said I could sit outside in the beer garden and she would bring it to me. So I did just that. As I sat down I heard a voice say: 'Ah don't be shy. Come and talk to me.'

I looked over to see a guy swaying in the corner with a pint of Guinness. 'No offence mate,' I replied, 'but it's shadier over here.'

'Ah well! I'll come to you then,' he said, and sauntered over.

Anton was originally from Dublin, but had lived here for the past twenty years.

'I don't want to go back to Dublin,' he told me. 'It's not the same anymore. All the kids I knew back then are now drug addicts.'

It seemed that of late Dublin's drug problem had spiralled out of control. Back in June 1996, the journalist Veronica Guerin was shot dead as she sat in her car at the traffic lights on a busy main road. She had been relentlessly pursuing the men behind the city's escalating drugs trade, and had persisted despite being shot in the leg on her own doorstep. However, her death was not in vain. It did spark the police into action and out of their defeatist attitude towards the dealers. The result was that the people she'd been chasing have now been put out of business.

Anton continued to relate these and other stories as he downed more pints, before finally loading a crate of twenty-four cans on the back of a small 125cc motorbike and riding off down the road with a slight swaying motion.

I wandered back to the hostel to find it had been invaded by a group of mentally handicapped men and women, who had arrived earlier in the day and were now having dinner in the kitchen. One man and one woman were supervising them all. It looked to be a full time job, too. One of them, who was a middle-aged man wearing a silver pin-striped suit one size too small and sporting a head of fiery red hair, started picking a fight with another. It began with an argument and ended with the red-haired man offering the other outside. The supervisor intervened and forced them both to sit down. The men were subdued for a moment. A short while later, the red-haired man started picking on someone else. Again the supervisor had to intervene.

Later on, as I was sitting in the common room, the red-haired man came in. When he saw me writing in my journal he came over.

'I write too,' he told me, quite proudly.

'Really.' I replied. 'What do you write?'

'Songs,' he said. 'Do you want to see one?'

I felt I had to say yes, or else he might pick a fight with me.

That night a group of lads came into the dorm at four in the morning and switched on the light, waking me up in the process. They then decided it would be fun to make lots of noise as they got ready for bed. I would have sorted them out, but they outnumbered me five to one. Now if my red-haired friend had been here, it would have been a different story.

Eventually the light went out and they all settled down to sleep. About bloody time. I turned over and settled back down again. The cloudy haze of sleep was about to engulf me once again, when from the beds next to mine came the most high-pitched bout of stereo snoring imaginable. The room was suddenly filled with the whistles and grunts of these two. It cut through me like a butcher's knife. I stuffed my head under the pillow and squeezed tight, but it still didn't drown it out. I had no choice but to put on my headphones and blast music into my ears, to avoid committing a double murder. I still couldn't sleep, but it was better than ending up with a life sentence.

I rose at eight and took great sardonic pleasure in noisily packing my bag. For a change I decided to take the train. The seating arrangements were much better than the trains at home. All the seats were situated around tables as opposed to rows of two. I got chatting to a nice old lady who had come from Dublin and was going to visit her son in Waterford. We talked about the current economic climate here in Ireland. It seemed that it was boom time here and they were crying out for skilled people. She said that Hewlett Packard had been advertising and that I should contact their branch in Bray, Co. Wicklow. It was worth a thought I suppose. My money was running low and I really wasn't all that keen on going home, yet.

My plan was to get to Tramore, a seaside resort twelve kilometres south of Waterford. I was going to surprise a friend. Three years before, I had worked with a bunch of other travellers for a month in Australia. We were recruited to renovate a hostel in Cairns. Amongst them was an Irishman. Paul came from Tramore and had given me his address. A month working and partying together had made us good friends. But as is usual when you part company, we failed to keep in touch. I have managed to keep in touch with a lot of the female friends I had made, but that's different; blokes don't really tend to write to each other. Therefore I was looking forward to meeting up with Paul again and reminiscing on our time in Oz, over a few pints.

As it was such a short distance I thought I'd hitch. But the sight of a row of buses waiting to leave for Tramore, and warning pains from my feet, made me get on one of those instead. Upon arrival I went off in search of the only hostel in town, *The Monkey Puzzle*. The puzzle was in finding it. I had tried to phone, but each time had got no answer. A man at the tourist information directed me up a steep hill and then left. I still couldn't find it, so I asked a passer-by. He pointed across the road to a house. 'I don't know where the sign has gone though,' he said.

I wandered up and rang the bell. There was no answer. I peered through the window. The beds were empty. I was about to leave when the door creaked open to reveal an over-weight char lady with a cigarette hanging from her mouth.

'Is this the hostel?' I asked her.

'Oh! We haven't been operating as a hostel for over two years now,' she replied.

'But two people directed me here, and didn't say anything about it being closed down. And one of them was the tourist information for the area,' I said.

It seemed that the locals here were a bit out of touch with current affairs.

I wandered back down to the main road and phoned Paul's number from a phone box, but got no answer. I ended up paying £16 for a B&B. It was nice to have a room to myself though. My room was white, and I mean white. In fact it was all white: the bedding, the walls and the furniture. It seemed that someone had had a surplus of white paint, or a worrying love for the colour. I put my sunglasses on and unpacked.

After a short walk around I phoned Paul again. This time his mother answered.

'Hi! Does Paul Tighe still live there?' I asked.

'Oh no!' came the reply. 'He's in Sligo!'

I couldn't believe what I was hearing. It seemed that Paul had gone back to university as a mature student. There had been something to keep me in Sligo after all. Whilst up in that neck of the woods, Anne had suggested that I phone and tell him I was coming. But I had wanted to surprise him. Looks like the surprise was on me.

My sole reason for coming to Tramore had been to see Paul again. With Paul being in Sligo, I found myself at a loss. Tramore was nothing more than a tacky tourist resort lined with expensive bars, restaurants and amusement arcades. My blisters were still playing me up, so a stroll along the coast was out of the question. Suddenly I hit upon an idea. In my backpack were some bags of Mexican jewellery that I had bought whilst travelling there a couple of years before: the result of much bargaining with the Indians. I always kept them with me on the off chance that I might be able to make a bit of money during my travels. I decided to set up along the beachfront.

I found a suitable spot on a wall and lay them all out on an Indian blanket. They proved to be extremely popular. As it was the weekend, and the sun was out, the place was packed. I made nearly forty pounds in a few hours.

Parked across from me was a caravan from which a woman was telling fortunes. Towards the end of the day she called me over. The sign out front read:

Madame Lisa "the oldest Gypsy in Ireland"

Madame Lisa said there was something in my face and that she wanted to read my fortune. I politely refused her offer, saying that I don't want to know my future. 'It's not because I'm a non-believer,' I told her. 'It's just that if something is going to happen to me, then I'd rather just let it happen. If I know it's coming then I will be spending my time looking out for it.'

As an example I said that if she told me I was going to marry a gorgeous brunette, then I would be expecting it to be every gorgeous brunette I meet. Now lets face it, there are a lot of gorgeous brunettes out there. Besides, the rest of the board out front read:

Fortunes read, "passed" and "presant"

If she couldn't even spell the words, then how could she tell me them? This didn't exactly instil me with a lot of confidence in her abilities. Nor did the fact that another caravan parked down the road also advertised fortune telling by Madame Lisa "the oldest Gypsy in Ireland".

The one advantage to a B&B is the breakfast. I made the best of it, as it was probably the only decent meal I would get in a while. The nice lady who owned the place let me leave my bag in her front room while I went off and tried to sell more jewellery. Business was a bit slower today. After four hours and eleven pounds I decided to quit. The weather wasn't quite as good either.

The bus stop was packed with day-trippers waiting to go back to Waterford. The next was at five. When five came three pulled up at once. To my horror they were local town buses and not the expressways I had hoped for. Expressways have luggage compartments underneath. These didn't. As I stood gaping, people pushed past me in fear of not being able to get on.

I asked the driver where I could put my pack.

'You'll have to take it to the back,' he replied.

As usual my tent prevented me from walking down the aisle. Sometimes I don't know why I bother taking it. I don't often use it, but it's handy as backup accommodation in times of trouble. I removed the pack, placed it on the floor and attempted to drag it up the aisle. However, now my daypack was causing problems, as it kept falling off my shoulder due to being only hooked over by one strap. The logical thing would have been to just put it on both shoulders properly, but people were piling up in front of me and I was starting to get flustered. This calls for drastic action, I thought. So I dumped my daypack on the poor unsuspecting couple next to me and said: 'Would you mind holding this for me?'

Without giving them a chance to answer, I dragged my pack to the rear of the bus and hoisted it up over the seats and into the boot. I then ran back down and retrieved my daypack from the rather bewildered, yet smiling, people I'd dumped it on.

Buses and backpacks just don't mix

The bus made a temporary stop right outside the hostel in Waterford, but I felt that if I subjected the passengers to this upheaval again, they might not be so accommodating this time. So I waited until we got to the station. When everyone had got off, I put on my pack and barged my way down the aisle. I really should get a smaller tent, I thought to myself. Especially when I realised how long I had to walk to get back to the hostel. This wasn't doing my sore feet much good at all.

The receptionist at the Viking Hostel had the most beautiful deep brown eyes. Once she had checked me in I had a short hobble around town. It seemed my blisters were getting worse. The price you pay for cheap boots, I suppose. Waterford is a beautiful city with narrow alleyways leading onto the larger streets. It's based around the river Suir's estuary. As this is deep enough to allow many modern ships right up to the city centre, Waterford is also a major shipping port. It's one of Ireland's busiest.

This situation with my feet was getting ridiculous. I decided that I had to stop and completely rest them up for a few days. I wondered if I could persuade the girl with the nice brown eyes to be my personal foot masseuse for the next few days. But the removal of my boots at bedtime put a stop to those thoughts. She seemed far too nice to subject to the pungent odours being excreted by those sweaty blisters. Also the hostel was big and rather impersonal. And there was no sofa in the TV room on which I could veg out for a few days. So I decided to go to Wexford the next day and stay there to convalesce, assuming the hostel was accommodating.

__18__

A Very Long Rest

Walking through the streets of Wexford Town I knew straight away that I had made the right decision. It is such an attractive town. The narrow, paved streets are lined with old historic buildings. There was only one hostel in town, *Kirwan House*. This was also a major feature in the Fridge Book. The author had stayed there and had sex in the owner's dog kennel.

I found the hostel up a tiny street just off of the Main Street. The door was answered by an old man sporting grey hair and an equally grey goatee beard. Behind his glasses sat large sunken eyes on a large oval-shaped face. It bore the lines of a man who had obviously seen a lot of life. He resembled an old eccentric painter. Éamonn had indeed seen a lot of life. He had been born in Ireland, but lived and worked in America for a long time. He taught underprivileged children in the ghettos of Chicago. Most were from Central and South America, predominantly Mexican. He was fluent in Spanish, which came in handy when he went to live in Madrid for a number of years. And he had also lived in Morocco. Éamonn had spent much of his youth in Ireland and had always loved it with a passion. But back in those days it wasn't such a prosperous place. Like many others, he'd had no choice but to seek work elsewhere. Now, it seemed, he wanted to see out his remaining days in the country he loved the most. And who could blame him?

It seemed I'd had the misfortune to arrive on the day when the hostel was always full. Every Monday the Paddywagon tour group came through and Butch, the owner, had struck a deal to let them stay at his place. So, for the first night at least, I had to pay extra for a room in a house down the road. Butch leased the building on a yearly basis. The rooms were mostly used for private, double or treble dorms. He charged an extra couple of pounds for the treble, which he put me in. I was directed up an extremely narrow stairway to the room.

I dumped my pack down and returned to the hostel for nice cup of tea and sat in the hostel's garden. There was a large patio with table and chairs and a small section of grass. I joined Butch and a friend on the grass. Butch was nursing a hangover and discussing his night out with his friend. I asked him where the doghouse was. 'It went with the girlfriend,' he replied.

Fifteen kilometres south of Wexford lies Rosslare Strand. It's an area of long, golden sandy beaches. I decided to spend the afternoon there. What better way to rest my feet than on a beach? Plus, the weather was gorgeous. I was now in the heart of the Sunny Southeast, and the day was warm. There were many things to do around Wexford, like visit the Johnstown Castle south of town, or the Irish National

Heritage Park to the north of town. But the lure of a nice sandy beach was much more appealing.

I decided to hitch down. Once I'd found what I thought to be a suitable spot for hitching, I began thumbing the passing traffic. One hour and one aching thumb later an old man, who had been standing across from me in a car park, came over.

'You'll not get picked up from here, it's not a good place for them to stop,' he said. 'You should go up that road to the outskirts of town.'

Why the hell didn't he tell me that before.

He gave me the necessary directions and I hobbled one kilometre up the road. So much for resting my feet.

No sooner had I found a spot and dumped down my day-pack than someone had stopped for me. Jack Kelly was driving an old brown Mercedes, and blimey could he talk! I had a job to get a word in edgeways. He explained that he was on his way back from dropping off his wife at the hospital. He didn't say why, and I didn't get a chance to ask. He called her his *mott*, and went on to explain that it was an old Dublin expression for wife. He dropped me at a turn off one kilometre from the beach. The road was too narrow to hitch and so I ended up walking. By the time I got to the beach my feet were burning, so I lay down and allowed the nice offshore breeze to cool them.

After spending a few hours lying on the sand I walked back to the junction and caught a lift with a priest. He took me halfway and from there I was given a lift from a roofer on his way home from work. The guy was slouched in the driver's seat and was very difficult to make conversation with. When he did speak I had a job hearing what he said. I was actually quite relieved when he dropped me off by the waterfront.

Back at the hostel I attempted to stay off my feet as much as possible. A bunch of people from the hostel were going out that night. I wanted so much to go with them, but I couldn't move. Instead I spent my first night in Wexford curled up in bed, and finished the Fridge Book.

The next morning I moved into a dorm at the main part of the hostel. I did nothing all day but put my feet up on the couch in the common room and watch daytime television. I personally believe that daytime television is specifically designed to send the sick back to work. It's just so mind-numbingly boring. I flicked through the channels and each one was just as bad. Here in Wexford it seemed, you could even pick up the British channels; or to be exact the Welsh versions of our channels. After a day of this I felt I really needed to get out before the build up of froth around my mouth caused concern for the other guests.

Throughout the day I had made a new bunch of friends from all over the world. That's the wonderful thing about hostels. Where else can you go out for an evening with a crowd of people like this? We had two Australians, an Israeli, a New Zealander, a Canadian, an Irishman, an Irish American and some Europeans. Éamonn took us all to the Tack Room to hear some traditional Irish music. Three men played by the window, and we all sat opposite them. The main singer and guitarist had the most incredible voice. It seemed that the Irish have a real talent for singing. There is a huge amount of talented musicians in this country.

Throughout my stay Éamonn never ceased to amaze me. He was in his mid-seventies and was still going to the pub with a crowd of people our age. The thing was though, nobody objected to him being there. He had this wonderful ability to be able to get along with everybody. And I mean everybody. Throughout my stay I witnessed him befriend everyone who entered that hostel. Each person instantly warmed to him. You couldn't help it. He had the talent of being able to tune in to wherever you were from and meeting you at that level. Butch best described it:

'Most of us can find a way to get through to eighty percent of the people we meet, and get along with them. But there are some that you just give up on. Éamonn gets through to that other twenty percent.

No matter where your interests lay, he could quite easily make conversation on that subject. During my stay I had some very insightful conversations with him. He also made me laugh a lot. He was the sort of wise old man you either wanted as your Grandfather, or want to be like when you get old. I wanted both.

The other person working in Kirwan House was Dave. Dave was a middle-aged Yorkshireman who also owned a boat. Along with running the hostel, he ran boat trips around Wexford harbour. The highlight of this trip was a view of Curracloe Beach where the D-day landings for *Saving Private Ryan* had been filmed. The film crew had stayed here for three months and put £16 million into the Wexford economy. Not bad going. The other highlight of the trip was viewing the seals. To do this Dave would negotiate his way through an extremely shallow sand bar. The majority of Wexford harbour is shallow, making it nice and warm for swimming. It forms the estuary for the River Slaney, the main river running through County Wexford. Over the years this river has deposited so much mud and silt in the harbour that this large and once thriving port is now too shallow for any major shipping to dock. Nowadays it's used for fishing and small boats. Much of the land has also been reclaimed and the waterfront pier and many of the buildings are now built where the water once was.

Thursday night was quiz night. A very attractive and extremely vibrant seventeen year old girl called Heather did the cleaning at the hostel. She was also very active with the Wexford Theatre Company. The quiz night was in aid of an upcoming production of Jesus Christ Superstar. Dave was there along with his friend, who bore an uncanny resemblance to Oliver Reed. It was then that I realised Dave looked like the British comedian Jasper Carrot. The two of them together were in total denial of their age. Nina, a Danish girl in her early twenties, had arrived at the hostel and come along on the quiz night. The two of them were slobbering over her like a couple of teenagers yet to have their very first sexual experience. Jasper Carrot and Oliver Reed out on the pull together, now there's an amusing thought.

A guy called Ross was also staying at the hostel. He was from County Waterford and had been working here for the past five months. From the hostel he had brought with him a German with an incredibly big and odd-looking goatee. It looked as though someone had stuck an offcut of beige carpet to his chin. The three of us were on Éamonn's team.

This evening I discovered the Kirwan House civil war. It seemed there was someone Éamonn didn't get along with: Dave. The feeling was mutual. As the quiz progressed Éamonn indicated – in the subtle way that I was to soon realise was one of his many talents – that we really should try to get a better result than Dave's team, or else he would never hear the end of it. However that didn't happen, and when it came to the final results Dave was delighted that his team had beaten Éamonn's, and took great pleasure in rubbing his nose in it.

After the quiz, Ross took Carpet Goat to another pub because he wanted to hear traditional music. I finished my drink and took Liz (the New Zealander) and Nina – much to Dave's disappointment, I'm sure – along with me to meet them. The music wasn't very traditional, but it was good and we caught the end of it. It seemed that the tradition of singing acapella at the end of the evening stretched beyond the boundaries of Inisheer. Two of the drinkers entertained everyone with a song of their choice. Again they were given centre stage. However, the men's voices weren't as sweet as the women's, so I didn't fall in love this time.

With my feet fully restored to normal I could quite easily have moved on. But quite frankly I felt no compulsion to. I liked it here. The town was nice, the hostel was clean, comfortable and friendly, and the weather was good. I set about catching a bus to Courtown for the day. It's a popular seaside resort and I figured it might make a good place to set up my newfound moneymaking stall. However, when I reached the bus station two things were against me: the bus timetable was wrong, and I had forgotten to bring my blanket. When I returned to the hostel, Butch suggested I set up outside the AIB bank on Main Street. I did, and made £45 in four hours. The great thing about selling jewellery is that it doesn't take up much room. I had around four hundred necklaces in a small bag, so it didn't weigh me down much.

With an income now, I decided that I was going to stay here in Wexford for the time being. In actual fact I ended up staying for a month. Something to do with the amount of pubs. Here's some interesting information for you. Wexford has a population of around 16,000. Someone also told me it has ninety-three pubs. With that many pubs there might be a chance of finding the Sisters of Murphy's.

That night the Corrs were playing at Lansdowne Road Stadium, just south of Dublin. After inquiries about tickets I deduced that I couldn't afford it. The tickets cost £27. I would also have to travel up there, stay overnight in Dublin and return. I was running short of money, and somehow I doubted that my little business would generate enough for a luxury such as this. On top of that there was no guarantee I would get a good view of Andrea. If I was going to a Corrs concert, then I would want to be so close to the front that I'd be drooling over her shoes.

I remained in town instead. I found the others in O'Faolains pub. At the back of the pub was a night-club, which opened at eleven. It was free if you were already in the pub. Otherwise you had to pay three pounds. We went through. The bar staff looked quite impressive the way they worked so fast. But as it transpired they were more fast than efficient. I gave the barmaid three pounds for a pint of Guinness and got £2.75 in change. Ross ordered two pints and got charged for one. His change was given to the person standing next to him. So it turned out to be quite a cheap night out.

I spent the rest of the month enjoying the fruits of Wexford town. I hitched a lift to Curracloe Beach for the day, then walked the incredibly long coastal walk back to Wexford. Curracloe lies just fifteen kilometres from Wexford and its beach is eleven kilometres long and backed by large sand dunes. It's just one of the string of magnificent beaches that line the Wexford and Wicklow coastline, and it has weather to match. For the whole month the weather was wonderfully sunny and warm. After my trek around the west of Ireland I could never have believed that such ongoing sunny weather could actually exist in this country. But exist it did.

I spent the month selling by day or taking coastal walks. In the evenings I would either go to the pub with the many different friends I was making in the hostel, or simply spend the evening in the comfortable hostel lounge watching TV and talking to guests, or having in-depth conversations with Éamonn. He was a very knowledgeable man and I never tired of talking to him. He was also fastidious about not wasting anything. He hated to see things, especially food, being thrown away unnecessarily. And he was right, really. In our modern world of abundant food we do actually waste a lot. Especially when it comes to backpacking. The easiest food to carry and cook is pasta. As a result, often too much pasta is cooked and thus much is left over. Éamonn would eagerly pounce on anyone about to throw away a bowl-full of cooked pasta and use it for himself.

My trip around Ireland was at an end. By the end of the month I didn't have much money left and needed to start earning some. My little stall was generating enough to live on, but that was all. As time went by my stock got smaller. Being as I got it in Mexico, I could hardly restock. So I went to Dublin for the day to look for work. I travelled for free, courtesy of Éamonn. At sixty-six Irish citizens get a free travel pass for all trains and buses. At seventy-five, if they have a physical disability making it difficult to get around on their own, they also get a companion pass, thus allowing someone to accompany them on their journeys. Éamonn was going to Dublin that day to find an old map of Wexford. He liked old houses and was trying to buy one in Wexford. I lost count of the amount of houses he looked at. When I eventually left the country he still hadn't decided on the one he wanted. Just when he'd narrowed it down to two, he would find another.

I spent my day registering with all the agencies in Dublin. They each expressed the same concern that I was only available for six months. The reason for this was that I planned to travel South America in the New Year. Ireland was indeed prospering, but they wanted to build up teams of skilled people. Therefore, they wanted people who would stay. Each agency promised to do what they could, though. But I didn't hold out much hope.

Shortly after, I was headhunted by a firm in England I'd often worked for. They were offering good money and a three-month contract. I was also being summoned home to meet my long lost aunt. Recently my dad had managed to track down his sister who he hadn't seen for over thirty years. She had moved to the States and they lost contact. She had come over to stay with him for five weeks. Of course by the time she arrived I was already in Ireland. They were going to come over to Wexford to see me, but circumstances put a stop to that. So I agreed to go back for a weekend before they went. Coupled with the offer of work, I decided I might as well stay.

And so, much to my disappointment, I started making plans to leave Wexford and Ireland. I really didn't want to go. Over the past two months I had grown to love this country with a passion. I loved the pace of life, the friendliness of the people, their passion for life and music, and their love for the Craic. The Craic is the Irish expression for fun. And it's possibly the most important expression in the whole of Ireland.

'How's the Craic?' No matter how bad things get, there's always the Craic.

The other thing about Ireland was that they hadn't lost touch with what is really important in life, people. The Irish will always be willing to go out of their way to help a fellow human being. Do someone a favour, and they will return the favour to someone else. It's a good philosophy, and one that should be adopted the world over. Aside from a few bad ones, everyone I had come across was more than willing to offer assistance where needed. Ireland is a nation where jealousy and paranoia hardly seemed to exist. They welcome strangers with a smile. I liked that.

In all of my past trips, my last night in the country wasn't really much to write home about. The trip had wound down and I was ready to go home. On my last night here though, I felt like I was leaving home. Whenever I go travelling I'm often treated to a leaving party in town by friends. This night I was treated to a leaving party by my friends here in Wexford. We started off in the Sky and the Ground pub. From the hostel came Éamonn, Butch, Liz and a few recent arrivals I had befriended. From Wexford came two guys I had made friends with while selling my Jewellery.

Ciarón was a street entertainer. He made his own puppets and put on shows in the street. He also made costumes and performed street mime. When I first met him he told me that he only drank cokes. When I met up with him in the pub later he was drinking Guinness. Over the next few weeks he proved to be quite a drinker. With him was Jez. Jez had been born in Ireland, but grew up in England. He made his living by busking - and would continue to until his band makes it big. He did quite well also. In the street he played many familiar tunes on the flute. The Irish people believe that if you are entertaining you should be rewarded for it. Hence they were much more giving than most other places. Jez told me about a time when he popped into the pub for one drink. He got talking to others there, and when he finished they asked him to stay.

'I'm sorry,' he said. 'I don't have much money.'

'Ah well! Play us a tune,' said the barman.

He did, and got a pint for it. When he had finished that, one of the other drinkers offered him the same courtesy. And so it continued until closing time.

I looked around me and savoured my last night in an Irish pub. I had great company and good Irish music to listen to. I also noticed something else: the people in this pub were of various ages, from youngsters to pensioners. Yet they weren't singled out into their relative age groups, like I would have expected, but were all mixing together. I suddenly realised that this had been a common sight in most of the pubs I had been in around the country. Where I come from it would be considered uncool to be hanging around with the older people. But here that didn't seem to be a problem, and youngsters quite happily laughed and joked and drank with them, without the slightest hint of embarrassment. I thought that was great.

As the evening progressed we all went off to another pub - all except Éamonn and Butch. At his age even Éamonn quite understandably wasn't up to partying all night with a group of youngsters. Butch and his girlfriend had other plans.

The rest of us partied the night away in Moonies, a bar down by the waterfront that stayed open until two. They didn't charge an entrance fee either. The Irish people's love for singing emerged once again this night. At the end of the evening Ciarón, Liz and I, in our drunken condition, started singing traditional folk songs. Suddenly a guy appeared from nowhere and joined in, while others were content to listen. Okay so none of us was exactly Christy Moore, but it was a Craic.

I finally staggered into my dorm at about three and managed to locate my bed in the corner. As I sat down I felt a lump. Someone was in my bed.

'You're in the wrong bed!' I told whoever it was.

'I'm sorry, I zought it was empty,' came a girl's voice with a very sweet French accent.

Oh well! I thought, I'm sure there's room enough for two. If I wasn't going to find the Sister's of Murphy's, then I could always use my newfound gift for coaxing and influencing without causing offence on this poor unsuspecting French girl. I had to get something out of kissing the Blarney Stone.

'Zat bed over zer is empty,' she continued, pointing to another across the room.

Hmm! I thought, well why didn't you use that? All my stuff was squeezed into the corner here. 'Well, I'll only have to disturb you early in the morning to get my stuff. I've got an early bus to catch,' I said.

She didn't answer. She was already fast asleep again. So much for my fair words and soft speech. Perhaps I should have used a bit of tongue when kissing the Blarney Stone? Still, I figured that as my bed sheets hadn't been changed for about two weeks, that would be punishment enough.

The next morning I lay on a bench at the back of the ferry and watched my adopted country shrink off into the distance. Many people who come to Ireland do so because they have Irish parents or grandparents, or were born there themselves. I had neither. I was born in England and so were my parents, grandparents and their parents. I had no Irish blood. I also had no intention of trying to be Irish, like many people that come here. All I wanted was to spend more time in Ireland and learn from these people all the things that had been lost in my country. When I was growing up England had seemed a lot like Ireland: friendly neighbours, laid back attitudes. I had also likened the stories my parents had told me about everyone gathering around the piano in the East End pubs of London and singing songs, to the pub life here in Ireland. I wasn't a big drinker – although after reading this book you might find that hard to believe. But it wasn't actually the drinking that had lured me to the pubs each night, but the atmosphere. I am a great lover of music, especially live music, so the music that is played there with such a passion was the real source of my love for this place. And all that, combined with the sunny weather here in Wexford, meant that although circumstances were making me leave, they wouldn't keep me away. And I vowed that one day soon I would return.

__Epilogue__

'Are ye goin ta appalagise far…?'

'Pardon!' I said.

'Are ye goin ta appalagise for de patay…?'

'I'm sorry I still didn't understand.'

He slumped further across the table and lifted his base-ball cap. 'Are ye goin ta appalagise fer de patayta famine?'

I was sitting in the Sky and the Ground three years after my first arrival in Wexford. My companions were two girls from the hostel, and one of them had befriended two drunks. She had introduced me to the one sitting next to me, and he in turn had introduced me to his even drunker friend across the table.

'Where ye from?' the man across the table had asked.

'England,' I replied.

Immediately he leapt up from his chair and attempted to assume a threatening posture without swaying too much. The man sitting next to me raised his hand and told him to sit down. He obeyed, reluctantly. He then lent across and asked me this absurd question, three times before I understood. Am I going to apologise for the potato famine? It wasn't what I expected.

'Well it's hardly my fault, now is it? I wasn't even born then,' I replied.

It was obvious that this man had clearly enjoyed one too many beers in his time. Every Guinness advert always depicts strong men doing manly things such as surfing gigantic waves or lifting immensely large objects; the slogan being: 'Guinness makes you strong' or 'Guinness for strength'. But in reality that's absolute rubbish. A little Guinness makes you strong, but too much Guinness makes you fat, forgetful of where you live and robs you of all self-dignity. Rather than carrying incredibly heavy objects home, you are more likely to crawl home unable to even carry yourself, or stagger your way through the streets bouncing off inanimate objects such as walls and lamp posts. You have trouble standing on solid ground, let alone a surfboard.

The Irish people have a right to hate the English, I suppose. After all, Britain hasn't been particularly nice to them in years past. But all that is political, and for the most I think the majority of the people don't really blame the everyday English visitor. This was actually the first time in all my years of coming to Ireland that I had experienced any hostility from a local. It was to be expected in any country.

There had been a recent news story in one of the tabloids. A French-Moroccan woman and her Irish husband had moved here from France. She had recently been subjected to a rare racially-motivated attack by three Irish women and was severely injured. She and her husband had announced that they were moving back to France and the husband had said: 'It seems we are no longer Ireland of the Welcomes.' The tabloid in question had splashed the words 'racist Ireland' in giant letters on the front page. This really disturbed me because Ireland is not racist. While it was a terrible thing that happened to this woman, it was an isolated incident and doesn't reflect the views of the Irish people. Ireland is going through a period of change. For the first time ever, Ireland is experiencing mass immigration because it is now more prosperous. Like any country experiencing immigration for the first time there is bound to be some who resent and fear strangers moving in. But they are often few and far between. Here in Wexford there had been a wonderful story about how the local people rallied round trying to fight a deportation order slapped on a woman and her young daughter from a third world country. The girl had been going to school here for the past few years and had made many friends. The locals wanted them both to stay and argued that taking the girl away from her friends back to a country that is alien to her, as she was just a baby when she came to Ireland, would be emotionally wrenching. I reckon that if you look hard enough you'd probably find many such stories and realise that this is what Ireland is really like. It's not 'racist Ireland'; it's still, and probably always will be, 'Ireland of the Welcomes'.

It had taken a year, but after vowing on that boat all those years ago to return, I did. I had come immediately back to Wexford. Kirwan House hadn't changed all that much, other than some new staff and guests. Instead of being greeted by Éamonn or Butch, my knock at the door was answered by a dark-skinned girl with bright, shining brown eyes and the widest smile I'd ever seen. Eva had the most convincing Irish accent, although she was in fact from Belgium. She soon turned out to be a bright and vivacious girl with a very expressive and quite quirky personality. She also became a very good friend.

Éamonn, to my delight, was still working there. In fact there would be no tearing himself away from the place. He loved working in Kirwan House and would probably do so for as long as he was able. I found him cooking in the kitchen and he greeted me with a hearty handshake. We then had lunch and Éamonn brought me up to date and told me all about his new house. He then introduced me to Richie from Wales, who was working in town, and would soon become a member of staff. We all went out to the Sky and the Ground for a few pints and some good Irish music.

It felt good to be back, like coming home again. I have travelled in a lot of places, and stayed in many backpacker hostels. Many have provided me with great memories. My favourite type of hostel is the small, homely hostels. Kirwan House is like that. It has a good kitchen, dining room and cosy television room. You can relax here and feel at home. And it has great staff who are very accommodating indeed.

I spent many happy months in Wexford over the following two years, and made some of my best friends there. I also noticed just how others arrived in Kirwan House and found it difficult to drag themselves away. All manner of people stayed there, from backpackers to small families with children. Kirwan House always attracted an eclectic crowd, and some extremely memorable and colourful characters. I watched the guestbook fill up with complimentary messages from many a satisfied guest. Many would come back. But one girl summed up Kirwan House and its staff perfectly. She called it 'the Kirwan House Big Family'. And how right she was.

If you're ever in town, be sure to pay it a visit.

To the End of the World and Back

A Millennium Adventure

Excerpt

At the bus station I bought a ticket for the midday bus to Punta
Arenas, Chile. I was about to enter a new country, only to leave
again shortly after. To get to Tierra del Fuego I would have to take
a boat from Punta Arenas. The island is unequally divided between
Chile and Argentina, one of the many arguments over land
between these two countries.

'Is it always so windy here?' I asked the girl at the counter.

'Yes,' she replied, 'cold also!'

The tone of her voice suggested that she longed to be elsewhere, preferably tropical.

She then presented me with a customs form to fill in, which
informs you of the various things you are not allowed to take into
Chile like: animals, vegetables, fruit and semen. *Semen!* How am
I supposed to help that? Perhaps I would be asked to remove it
before entry. I imagined arriving at the border and being directed
to join a long line of men, eventually leading to a door where a
nurse would be handing out magazines.

To the End of the World and Back (A Millennium Adventure)

Reviews

South East Voice, Ireland's Free Newspaper, 29 November 2001.

It's one thing to have been immersed in such an experience as Ian's, quite another to reproduce it for the reader so vividly that you can virtually visualise the magic of each moment. In telling this story Ian brings many enviable gifts to his task; an ability to tell a multi-faceted story in a fluid, coherent narrative form; a sardonic wit; an eye for comic detail and gift for consistently transporting the reader to the heart of his experiences.

If you are looking for an exciting and enthralling story told with an extraordinary clarity, this book is for you.

Angela Turnball, Salisbury Journal, 4 April, 2002.

Through desolate and spectacular landscapes, from sea level to the heights of Bolivia, Ian's account of his adventures and misadventures is always engrossing.

This is a travel book that passes the ultimate test – you wish you were there too

A Reader's review

I picked up my copy at the Independent Travellers Exhibition in London where Ian's photographic display of his expeditions caught my eye. His book is an inspiring, raw account of the humorous and taxing trials of a financially challenged and incident-induced global expeditioneer. Ian Middleton illustrates an honest, blatant view of backpacking life, giving an insight to the fundamental reasons why we love to traipse into the unknown mysteries of cultural diversification and unimaginable lands. 'To the End of the World and Back' is packed with beauty and culture that not only re-captured my personal appreciation for South America, but also rejuvenated my interest to visit other places I had not. I will definitely be going back to catch up with Fernando!!.

Carl Woodman. International Kiwi.

Read a sample chapter from the forthcoming book.

Down Mexico Way

__Two Exits and No Waiting Please!__

We arrived in the afternoon and went into the actual town of Palenque before finding a campsite. The town itself was quite run-down. We parked up the van and went in search of supplies. Walking down the street we spotted a waiter excitedly gesturing us to come up to his restaurant. So we did. We were the only people there. The absence of people in a restaurant always makes me wonder if they know something I don't. But we were there now so we sat down and had a meal. I ordered a torta with a plate of chips and a banana and orange licuado; a licuado is a popular drink consisting of a blend of fresh fruits of your choice. However, the licuado came with ice. I didn't have faith in the owner for having used purified water, so I removed them. The one downside to travelling with Efrain was that he was an American and used to tipping, so he would always leave a good tip. This made me feel that I should too. Being a budget traveller, this was not something I would have normally done.

We were now in the state of Chiapas. About two kilometres from the ruins we found a great campsite. I put up my tent for Efrain and Zonelle to sleep in, and Devon and I hung our hammocks under a palapa. This is basically a wooden shelter with a palm-thatched roof where you could hang hammocks and sleep sheltered from the rain, but in the open-air. I wondered if the one we had chosen would leak. After setting up our beds for the night, we settled down for the evening with some nice cold beers.

Our experience so far in the tropical lowlands of the Yucatán Peninsula had taught us the warning signs of an approaching storm. Naturally there was the sound of distant thunder, but what told us that it would head our way was the trees. In the still air, the leaves of the trees would occasionally rustle and gently flutter, but we would feel no breeze at all. Again it was amazing because this would continue for about an hour, and it would never get any stronger. The leaves would flutter as gently as they had the previous time. It was like a whispered warning from the storm itself. Then it would sweep in and engulf you before you even had a chance to start running for shelter.

When the storm blew in we all ran to our respective shelters. People scattered in all directions like startled horses. I was happy to see that our palapa didn't leak. I lay in my hammock and was halfway through my last bottle of beer when I started to feel a bit queasy. I figured that I'd just had one too many, and so threw the remainder away and climbed into my hammock and tried to sleep. This proved a bit difficult because Devon was next to me and I felt certain he was a bit scared. It was very dark where we were and we couldn't even see each other, despite the fact that we were virtually side by side. All around the campsite was thick, tropical jungle. From deep inside that jungle emitted the many sounds of the animals that lived there. This could be quite unnerving, especially to an eight-year old boy. Devon kept talking to me, probably checking to make sure I was still there and hadn't been silently dragged off by some beast of the night. I tried to stay awake for as long as I could, hoping he would eventually settle and go to sleep. But I think that I fell asleep before him because when I awoke during the night he was gone. I guessed that he had gone to the tent. I couldn't blame him really, the sounds of the jungle could be quite spooky.

*

I was awoken in the morning by a strange bodily feeling. It was almost as if somebody was inside banging on the rim of my stomach with a hammer and shouting: *'Everything out, two exits and no waiting please!'*

I fell out of the hammock and sped across the field to the toilet, clenching my cheeks in the process.

This was all I needed!

I remained there on the toilet until I was sure that my bowels were sufficiently drained. This was not an uncommon experience to me, but it was the worst yet. In fact I made several trips back to the toilet before we headed off to the ruins. By the time we left I was feeling extremely ill. Not only was my bottom twitching and my throat constantly threatening to erupt like a volcano, but also my body was completely drained of all energy, and every joint ached.

We went into town first for breakfast. This wasn't a good idea for me because even the mere mention of food in Spanish sent me running to the toilet. The walls to the restaurant toilet were made out of thin plywood and obviously didn't provide much sound-proofing. I would have felt pity for the poor people having to listen to these sounds emitting from inside as they ate, but I was too busy concentrating on alternating between top and bottom without causing spillage. After a while I began to wonder where it was all coming from. It felt like enough fluid had been extracted from my body to fill a small swimming pool. I certainly couldn't have drunk that much, so my body must have been calling upon reserve fluids. I had visions of all the moisture being sucked out of my skin in order to flush out this deadly foreign matter that was invading my body. And with all the weight I must be losing, I would stagger out of the toilet looking like the old man from Steptoe and Son, shouting, *'Efrain!'*

I finally emerged from the toilet looking somewhat paler than before. I was about to walk off when I heard a whistle. I turned to see the waiter gesturing for me to close the toilet door.

You bloody do it! Can't you see I'm dying here?

I turned and closed the door, not having the energy to argue, and then staggered back to the table. The waiter, obviously either sympathetic to my ailment or not wanting any more of his customers subjected to those sounds again, offered me a cup of herbal tea.

I assumed this to be the end of it because I couldn't possibly have had anything more inside me. In fact I could have sworn that I was missing a few minor organs. As the others tucked into their cooked breakfasts I sipped my tea and tried not to look, and also wondered if I should tell them that the kitchen had been right behind the toilet? But I thought it best not to. After all, ignorance is bliss, isn't it?

When we got to the ruins I felt like I was at death's door, but I was determined to go in. I had waited a long time to see these ruins and wasn't about to miss my chance. I staggered into the park feeling like an old man. I could have made good use of a Zima frame. However, I only made it as far as the bottom of the Temple of Inscriptions before my body started emitting the warning signs of yet another evacuation.

The toilet was outside the park by the ticket office. I realised that I would have to pay to go back into the ruins, but in all honesty I doubted if I had the energy. To climb those pyramids when feeling fit was quite a feat, but to attempt it when feeling like this was nothing short of suicide. I had left Efrain and co in the park and he had the keys to the van, so I couldn't go there. I spotted a bench outside the toilets and gratefully sat down. But even to sit proved too much of an effort, so I lay down. The bench was made of solid hardwood and wasn't the most comfortable place on which to lie, but I didn't have much of a choice. It's at a time like this when you realise just how unconcerned people can be with someone they don't know. There I was lying pale-skinned on that bench, slipping in and out of consciousness, and judging by the looks I was getting the people were obviously annoyed that I had the audacity to do it in a public place, and stop others from sitting down.

I lay there for what seemed like an eternity. When the others finally returned I told them that I wanted to go back to the campsite. Before I went back though, we went in to town and I got Zonelle to buy me a big bottle of water and a big packet of salted crackers. I had to try to re-hydrate myself.

Back at the campsite I headed straight for the luxury of my hammock and spent the afternoon nibbling crackers and sipping water in-between sleeping. I couldn't believe my bad luck. I had come so close to seeing the famous lid of Palenque, and had been viciously struck down by bad Mexican food. I assumed it was the meal in that scummy restaurant upon arrival that had caused this. I wanted revenge on that waiter. The next day we would be leaving and I would never see the lid of Palenque. I started to wonder if I should stay on, assuming that I felt better the next day, and try to meet up with the others at San Cristóbal de las Casas. But as luck would have it I didn't need to.

I say luck, but it wasn't really for Efrain and Zonelle. When they returned from their trip out that afternoon, Efrain informed me that he was having problems with the clutch in his van. The next day they went into town to try and get it fixed. I was feeling a lot better and offered to take Devon to the ruins with me, to save him having to hang around while the van was being fixed. He had found some tunnels in one of the ruins the day before and had wanted to explore them, but didn't have a torch. So he was quite keen to go back with me. This time he made sure that he took a torch with him.

From Palenque minibuses ran to the ruins on a regular basis, so we crossed the road outside the campsite and waited for one. Also waiting there were three English girls. We got talking and Devon made quite an impression on them. Each time a minibus passed it was full and wouldn't stop. I began to get fed up with waiting and stuck out my thumb in the hope of hitching a lift. It worked. A pickup truck pulled over and the five of us climbed in the back. It was a much more fun ride than the bus.

At the ruins Devon was all excited about going to the tunnels.

I told him not to rush me as the illness the previous day had taken a lot out of me, and I hadn't fully recovered. I also pointed out that the first thing I wanted to do was see the tomb of Pakal. This was located deep inside the pyramid. First I had to climb the sixty-nine steps to the top of the pyramid, then descend a very steep stairway. On top of this, the inside of the pyramid was extremely humid, which made the stairs very wet and slippery. A long queue also lined these steps and it took a while to get there. Devon got fed up waiting and went back outside. When I finally got to the tomb I discovered that the room was closed to the public and the lid could only be viewed through the doorway, which made it quite difficult to get a good look. I was furious! After all that effort I was denied the chance to study it up close.

This crypt had laid undiscovered until 1952 when a man named Ruz Lhuillier, who had been excavating the staircase, found a sealed passageway with skeletons seated inside. They were the victims of a religious sacrifice intended to serve Pakal in death. The skeletons were buried with clay pots, jewellery and tools for his journey to the next world. Pakal's jewel-adorned body and the priceless jade mosaic death mask he wore were removed and placed in a replica of his tomb in the Museum of Anthropology in Mexico City. The tomb and lid remain here because it is impossible to remove it. (The temple was built around the sarcophagus.) The giant stone lid contains an image of Pakal surrounded by serpents, mythical monsters, the sun god and glyphs recounting Pakal's reign. It was without doubt a magnificent piece of work. It was intricately carved. This was the first crypt to ever be found in Mayan pyramids and gave way to speculation that they may actually be related to the peoples of Ancient Egypt. But how did they get here? Once such theory is that they were all descendants of the lost world of Atlantis. Whoever they were or wherever they came from, they obviously thought a lot of this bloke Pakal to go to all the trouble of building an entire pyramid around him.

When I re-emerged on top of the pyramid Devon allowed me a few minutes rest before insisting that we go and explore the tunnels he had found. We ventured up a hill and through a small opening. To Devon's disappointment it was just a group of small passageways that weren't very long. There were no hidden stashes of gold or treasure, just some very unusual smells.

As we emerged back out into the sunlight I spotted some Indian ladies selling coconuts. They appeared to be speaking to each other in their native language. This was the first time I had heard that. Sitting in a group near to them were some people dressed in white robes and generally looking at peace with Mother Nature. I was particularly interested in the woman going around the group with a metal bar that when hit, emitted a resonating frequency. She was then radiating this frequency over each person in turn. When she spotted Devon and I watching, she asked us if we wanted to try. 'It's very relaxing,' she said.

And she was right.

We sat and talked with them for a while. They were nice people, a little weird, but nice. They were part of a club in the United States that arranged trips to places like this in order to 'feel the energy.'

Whatever takes your fancy.

One woman proceeded to read Devon the Mayan equivalent of his birth sign whilst another drew him the Mayan symbols relating to this. He was quite chuffed at that.

Back at the campsite we spent the rest of the day in the swimming pool. Zonelle came later and picked up Devon. It seemed there was a serious problem with the van and they would be staying at a hotel in town. They needed a certain part and the garage didn't have it. At worst they would have to order it from the States, which could take ages. She told me where they were staying and I arranged to come and see them in the morning. I opted to stay at the campsite, as it was only fifteen pesos per night.

The next day I took a bus into town and found their hotel. As luck would have it they had found the necessary part and fixed the van. Efrain had worked on it with the mechanics in the garage, as that was his profession at home. They had told him they only earned fifty pesos a day, which was the equivalent of about four pounds. Christ, I thought, I would want more than that for an hour's work.

The previous evening Efrain had suffered the same illness as me. There was definitely something seriously bad about the food in this town. Mind you, with them having the toilets next to the kitchen, I suppose it's to be expected. After loading up the van and then retrieving my stuff from the campsite, we headed off for our next destination.

Author's note

'Where are the Cotswolds?' I asked my work colleague as we ate our lunch.

'What!' he exclaimed in surprise. 'A traveller like you doesn't know where the Cotswolds are?'

'Well, I've never been there,' I replied.

It's a mistaken belief that someone who travels knows the world. I have lived most of my life in the UK, but really know nothing about it. I only know my hometown. Even then I don't really know the town, I just know of my experience of it. The same applies to my books. These are not representations of the countries I travel; they are just my impressions and experiences of them. I make no pretence of knowing them. I just want to share my experience and adventures with the reader. I hope it will inspire others to do likewise. Everybody can and should travel in some form or another. It's an enlightening and highly amusing experience, and certainly not as dangerous as people imagine (You only hear of the people who do get killed or hurt, never about the thousands who don't). The expression 'travel broadens the mind' couldn't be truer. I implore you all to get out of your seats and see somewhere other than your own hometown, even if it's in your own country, or a neighbouring one. I have travelled many distant and exotic places like Mexico, Australia, Hawaii and South America. When I announced to people that I planned to go to Ireland, their astonished reply was: 'Ireland, that's not very far!' Yet I found Ireland equally, if not more fascinating than all the other countries I had been to. The moral is that you don't need to go far, or for long, to experience the wonders of travelling. Just do it. I hope you enjoyed this book, and any others I write. But most of all, I hope it made you laugh.

Visit my website: **www.ian-middleton.co.uk**